Getting Started in Theatre

Getting Started in Theatre

Linda Pinnell

Fairmont Senior High School
Fairmont, West Virginia

National Textbook Company
a division of NTC/CONTEMPORARY PUBLISHING GROUP
Lincolnwood, Illinois USA

Cover photographs: Dawn Murray, Theatre and Interpretation Center, Northwestern University, Evanston, Illinois

Acknowledgments for literary material and interior photographs are on p. 119, which represents a continuation of the copyright page.

ISBN: 0-8442-5773-7

Published by National Textbook Company,
a division of NTC/Contemporary Publishing Group, Inc.,
4255 West Touhy Avenue,
Lincolnwood (Chicago), Illinois 60646-1975 U.S.A.
8 9 0 VL 9 8 7 6 5 4 3

Contents

Preface

Theatre is a unique art form that took root in ancient ritual and has grown to encompass every human emotion from grief to euphoria. While theatre has evolved constantly in the past twenty-five centuries, there is one element that has remained constant, the connection established between the action on stage and the audience.

Drama is the only literature written specifically to be performed before an audience. Because of this, to truly appreciate the form, you must understand all of the components that move the play from page to stage.

This book is your introduction to a very complex world, a guide to *getting started in theatre*. Each chapter covers a different element of theatre and gives you background information and activities designed to get you involved in drama and theatre.

- Chapter 1 provides a brief history of theatre and more fully explains what separates drama from other types of literature.

- Chapter 2 analyzes the form in more detail, differentiating between the major types of drama.

- Chapter 3 and Chapter 4 focus on the technical aspects of theatre including set design, lighting, props, costumes, and makeup.

- Chapter 5, Chapter 6, and Chapter 7 focus on the actor's role in the production. Along with discussing styles of acting, the elements of stage movement and vocal interpretation are detailed.

- Chapter 8 and Chapter 9 discuss the role of the director and give an overview of the entire rehearsal process.

- Chapter 10 is a collection of scenes from a wide variety of plays, offering you opportunities to experiment with strategies for performance and production you learn throughout the text.

All of the chapter activities will get you thinking about theatre. Some activities are writing exercises; some may be assigned as homework, at your teacher's discretion. Many will require physical and emotional participation in class, culminating in performance before an audience.

A glossary of key theatre terms introduced in this text and an appendix on career opportunities in the theatre are included at the end of this text.

1 What Is Drama?

A Brief History of Theatre

Most people cherish childhood memories of having stories told or read to them. In the jumble of Mother Goose, Peter Rabbit, folklore, Dr. Seuss books, and tales about your heritage that your family and teachers shared with you, certain stories stand out—stories that became favorites to be listened to over and over again.

Often the appeal of these tales came not from the stories themselves, but from the person who told them. Maybe Dad did all the voices when he read *The Cat in the Hat*. Maybe Grandma brought Harriet Tubman and the underground railroad to mind in dramatic detail. Maybe no one built the suspense of Cinderella's trying on the glass slipper like the library's storyteller could.

As you grew older, you began to realize that different people could tell the same joke with varying degrees of success. You realized that there is an art to telling a story. "It's not in the tale," the saying goes, "it's in the telling."

Activity One

Your teacher will divide the class into groups of three or four. Each member of the group will tell the others a story. These stories may be fairy tales, jokes, or real-life experiences. At the conclusion of all the stories, each group should choose one person to tell his or her story to the entire class. Listen carefully to these presentations and discuss what makes these students good storytellers.

The earliest literature evolved from the oral tradition, literature not written down but passed by word of mouth from generation to generation. This tradition crosses many cultures. The African *griot* (oral historian), the revered Native American story-tellers, the anonymous author of the Old English tale *Beowulf,* and the ancient Greek poet Homer all are or were talented, dramatic storytellers—so great that their stories survive through centuries.

1

As a child, once you got beyond the listening stage, you probably began making up your own stories. Your play sessions may have been reenactments of your favorite movies or TV shows—or maybe they were on-the-spot improvisations—but you loved assuming another character and pretending to be someone else.

Activity Two

What was your favorite game of pretending when you were a child? What made it so much fun? What props were involved? Who were your playmates? What was the setting for your game? The old West? A tropical island? A battlefield?

The Beginning in Ancient Greece

Given the universal human love of sharing stories and taking on other identities, it seems inevitable that these elements would eventually merge into a formalized *genre*, or type of literature. This happened in the fifth century B.C. in Athens. The ancient Greeks became the first people in the Western world to present to an audience familiar stories in a formal manner. Although the ancient Greeks were the creators, ancient Greek theatre bears little resemblance to theatre as you know it today.

Drama began as a religious rite to the god of wine, Dionysus. You easily can feel the religious overtones in Greek drama, especially the tragedies.

Originally, the plays were chanted by a chorus of fifty men. Eventually, Thespis, a Greek playwright, had one member of the chorus step out from the group and assume the role of a character. Thus, the first actor was added to the concept of theatre. Aeschylus, a writer of tragedy or a *tragedian* added the second actor; and Sophocles, another dramatist, added the third. Finally, the characters could converse in a crude type of dialogue. However, the addition of dialogue did not mean the end of the chorus. The chorus was still there, often representing the elders of the city or even the major character's conscience, interpreting the action, foreshadowing what was to come, and summarizing what had gone before.

Other unique aspects of Greek theatre were the direct result of compromises needed to perform the plays in huge open-air amphitheatres. Although theatres seating thousands of people are fairly common today, they are designed to acoustical perfection, with balcony seating and elaborate lighting to allow the audience to see and hear the action. The Greeks built tiers of seats up a hillside. The appearance of these early theatres was much more like a stadium as we know it than a theatre.

Activity Three

Brainstorm for a minute. If you were told that the school play would have to be canceled unless it were performed in the gymnasium or the football stadium, what would you do?

So how did these early performers overcome the obstacles in the days before sound systems and electrical lighting? With typical Greek ingenuity.

Obviously, plays were performed only in daylight, but there were also more elaborate and innovative solutions. Under their robes, actors wore *cathurni,* high platform shoes that added almost an extra twelve inches of height. Another bit of costuming that added to the actor's larger-than-life visibility was the *mask.* From a great distance, the bare face, even the heavily made-up face, would be lost. The mask portrayed character to the distant seats of the amphitheatre. What's more, the mouthpiece of the mask appears to have been a resonating chamber, a kind of megaphone, to help project the voice.

Greek Tragedy

One more thing aided the Greeks' comprehension of the plays. Typical of the epic and most early forms of literature, the dramas were based on familiar plots. These plots revolved around well-known characters and often followed a family of characters through several generations in a *trilogy,* or series of three plays.

Because the audience already knew the plots and characters of the Greek tragedies, there were no element of suspense, no plot twists, and no surprise endings. Instead the audience experienced what the philosopher Aristotle referred to as *catharsis,* the spiritually cleansing effect of good tragedy. Think about the last movie you saw where you were totally caught up in the tale and identified thoroughly with the main character's misfortune, then left the theatre feeling renewed. That was a catharsis.

Activity Four

What is your all-time favorite movie? If it is a sad movie, what is its appeal? Why do audiences flock to movies that are sometimes referred to as "tear-jerkers"?

Ancient Comedy

Once theatre was born, it grew rapidly and evolved continuously. One of its first innovators was Aristophanes, a contemporary of Sophocles. It is easy to see tragedy, with its solemn, moral tone, as an expression of religious rites. But Dionysus, the god of drama, was also the god of wine and fertility whose rites often degenerated into destructive chaos. Aristophanes picked up on another side of human as well as Dionysian nature in the development of comedy.

While the chorus was still a part of Greek comedy, its members were now costumed as clouds or birds or wasps. The action of comedy was fast moving and physically broad. No topic was off limits for Aristophanes's sharp, irreverent sense of humor; politics, sex, bodily functions, and prominent Athenians were all part of his comic domain.

Perhaps the most important thing about Aristophanes was his total originality. No longer was the writer limited to time-worn stories of ancient heroes. Playwrights could turn their attention to contemporary stories and characters.

Still, as Aristophanes found out, theatre is a reflection of its era. When the Athenian democracy fell, the new succession of tyrants would not allow his no-holds-barred brand of ridicule. Aristophanes and his later contemporary Menander softened the pointed, satiric barbs and retreated to a kind of domestic comedy, employing characters like the bumbling father, the nagging wife, and the sly servant. The characters were refined by the Roman playwrights Plautus and Terence, and these comic characterizations later spread throughout Europe in *commedia del l'arte,* a special form of comedy. These stock characters are still identifiable in today's situation comedies on television and in films.

Activity Five

Certain one-dimensional characters from early comedy prevail today. Describe the following or cite examples from recent movies and TV shows.

1. The young couple in love
2. The cantankerous old man
3. The nagging wife
4. The clever servant
5. The pretentious scholar

The Middle Ages

Since theatre does reflect its era, it is constantly changing to suit the tastes of a particular audience. In some eras, theatre seemed to cease altogether. The period between the fall of the Roman Empire and the onset of the Middle Ages seems geared more toward the epic than the drama. Epic poems were recited from memory in the oral tradition, rather than being performed in a dramatic sense.

The Middle Ages, with its dread of the plague, produced little theatre. Few people of that era desired to be all in one place as part of a large audience. Still, professional commedia troupes traveled from village to village, performing improvised playlets with characters reminiscent of the ancient comedies. Groups of laborers who belonged to the same guild performed plays based on stories familiar to them, often from the Bible. These short plays eventually evolved into a form called *morality plays* in which virtues and vices are personified as characters. The most famous of these, *Everyman,* is still performed and read today.

The Renaissance of Drama

By the 1500s, these stubborn little patches of theatre had laid the groundwork for the Renaissance dramatists, most notably Shakespeare and Molière. This Renaissance, literally a rebirth, meant going back to knowledge and ideas of earlier time periods. Nowhere was this rebirth more evident than in theatre. During Queen Elizabeth's reign, William Shakespeare, acclaimed the greatest of all English playwrights, had a most appreciative audience. People of Elizabethan England—from the nobility in the private boxes to the peasants who paid a penny to stand in the pit, the area around the stage platform—flocked to the theatre. And Shakespeare's plays appealed to all of them. Similarly, other European nations saw a renewed interest in drama. In France, the comic genius of Molière refined the "flat" stereotypical characters of the "commedia" into masterpieces of humor.

Theatre from the Restoration Through the 1800s

After Oliver Cromwell came to power in England in 1649, the popularity of theatre waned, due to the politically influential Puritans who believed theatre was sinful and sought to close down all performances. However, the theatre erupted again when King Charles II was restored to power. The drama of the Restoration Period in England in the early 1700s was filled with rollicking good humor and satire. At the same time, theatre in France retained a very formal and traditional format.

During the reign of Queen Victoria in England through the late 1800s, a period typical for its reservedness or "stuffiness," playwrights like Oscar Wilde perfected the *comedy of manners*. The comedy in these plays arises from the characters' responding to ludicrous events with well-bred gentility, totally at odds with the situation.

At the same time in other parts of the world, totally different approaches to drama were being taken. For instance, writers such as August Strindberg of Sweden and Henrik Ibsen of Norway were experimenting with the concept of *realism;* that is, these writers made their plays so realistic, it was as if an audience were eavesdropping and watching the action on stage through an invisible fourth wall. Being one of the first writers to address social problems in his plays through the effective use of realism and symbolism, Ibsen is considered the father of modern drama.

In the United States, theatre was beginning to flourish in the late 1800s with the popularity of minstrel shows, vaudeville, and—in particular—*melodramas*. American audiences at the turn of the century adored these overblown, larger-than-life dramatizations of black-caped villains and heroines like Little Nell, viewed with amusement by audiences today.

An Overview of 20th Century Drama

The prewar days of the early twentieth century found Americans almost in a frenzy as their thirst for theatre grew and grew. Stage/set designers such as Adolphe Appia (Switzerland) and Gordon Craig (England) made new advances in stagecraft, such as revolving stages and multiple sets. Modern American theatre was developing.

With the end of World War I in 1918, an era ensued that was complex, filled with disillusionment along with a diverse and international mix of ideas; nowhere was this mix more evident than in the theatre. American writers such as Susan Glaspell, who was an early feminist voice in 1916 with the production of her one-act play

Trifles, and Eugene O'Neill, the foremost playwright of the early part of the twentieth century with such plays as *The Iceman Cometh,* were primarily realists. However, they and their counterparts in the United States and around the world experimented with other dramatic forms.

The theatre of the absurd, which began in France with the plays of Samuel Beckett and Eugène Ionesco, was one form of experimental theatre that became popular in the 1950s and 1960s. This style of drama, based on *absurdism,* went against the traditional concepts of plot, character, and dialogue, reflecting the chaos and unpredictability of the modern world.

Another and very different aspect of modern theatre was the emergence of the musical. Beginning in the 1940s, the American collaborative teams of Rodgers and Hammerstein and Lerner and Loewe began producing dozens of upbeat, feel-good musical comedies, which see frequent revivals on Broadway (the best-known center of the professional theatre in the U.S.), and play almost nonstop in touring companies, community theatres, and school productions. Today, it seems Andrew Lloyd Webber of England has become the master of the musical drama with such hits as *Cats, The Phantom of the Opera,* and *Aspects of Love.*

A look at recent Pulitzer Prize-winners for drama reveals the diversity of contemporary American theatre. Marsha Norman won a Pulitzer Prize for *'night, Mother* (1983), a powerful Broadway play about a mother–daughter relationship and suicide. In 1989, Wendy Wasserstein won a Pulitzer Prize for *The Heidi Chronicles,* a drama demonstrating the playwright's mastery of humor in the story of one woman's life.

Another dramatization of the diversity of American theatre today is the fact that August Wilson, an African American playwright, has become a major voice in contemporary theatre with two Pulitzer Prize-winning dramas—*Fences* (1987) and *The Piano Lesson* (1990). Increasingly, minority playwrights—Luis Valdez and David Henry Hwang, to name just two—are being recognized with critical acclaim as well as commercial success.

The Future of the Theatre

Each season opens its doors to new dramatic forms and new issues, reflecting the desires and concerns of our global society as we approach the twenty-first century.

Competing with radio, television, and film, theatre as an art and entertainment form has been challenged. Critics have decried the death of theatre for years, but it is difficult to believe that any art form that has adapted, changed, and flourished throughout the centuries is even close to its final death knell.

Today in any major city, and even in some smaller towns, you may choose from a wide variety of theatrical experiences—from the classics to new plays being produced for the first time. When you add in movies and television along with live theatre, viewing options become limitless. Theatre will continue in both traditional forms and forms yet to evolve because it addresses the basic human need to share stories and universal experiences.

2 Types of Drama

The Play's the Thing—Hamlet

Drama is different from any other form of literature in that it is written as dialogue and intended to be performed for an audience. A novel by Dickens or Hawthorne remains static, unchanging. It is exactly as the author wrote it over a century ago. But no two productions of *Hamlet* are exactly the same, partially because of what the directors, actors, and technicians bring to the performance, but also because of the audience. Theatre is vibrant, alive, always changing. Yet every production needs a starting point, a script, a written format. Even Shakespeare's Hamlet agreed; "The play's the thing."

The Dual Nature of Drama

The universal logo for theatre is the masks of comedy and tragedy. It is interesting to note that most often these masks are in some way joined, indicating that comedy and tragedy are not separate entities but parts of the same whole, overlapping frequently. Shakespeare realized this and frequently overlapped his comic and tragic elements. After Macbeth's murder of Duncan, he provides the audience with the drunken porter. Hamlet converses with two punning gravediggers at the site of a newly dug grave, not yet realizing it is for his beloved Ophelia. Likewise, many comic writers include scenes of true sentiment and poignancy.

In the early 1980s television producers attempted to describe certain new shows as "dromedies," an odd hybrid of comedy and drama. These were basically situation comedies that attempted to handle serious issues with no laugh track. The term never caught on, probably because many dramatists have combined these elements for centuries.

Although there is a tremendous overlap between various forms, there are still terms that may help to delineate the most frequently encountered types of drama.

Tragedy

The earliest form of drama is *tragedy,* which comes from the Greek word *tragoedia,* meaning "goat song." This unusual derivation may come from the tradition of a sacrificial goat being offered to the glory of the winner of ancient Athenian competition. Greek tragedies were unique in their use of a chorus to respond to and interpret the action of the play.

The traditional tragic format was popular for centuries, well through the time of Shakespeare. Although later tragedians did not rely on a chorus, certain aspects of tragedy have remained intact. A traditional tragedy revolves around a single character, the tragic hero. According to tradition, a *tragic hero* must have two qualities; he must be a person of great stature, and he must fall victim to a *tragic flaw* in his own personality. Although there are exceptions, such as Antigone and Medea, the tragic hero was most often a male. He was often a king, such as Oedipus. Even as late as Shakespeare's day, fitting tragic heroes were a prince (Hamlet), a king (Lear), or an ambitious nobleman (Macbeth). The idea that the common man could be heroic or his destruction tragic is a much more recent idea, one dependent upon the ideal that "all men are created equal."

Although the tragic hero may seem to be swept along by circumstances beyond his control, there is some aspect of his own personality that contributes to his downfall. Whether it is Oedipus's stubborn desire to know the truth, Hamlet's inability to take action or Macbeth's vaulting ambition, the tragic flaw is at least partially to blame.

Activity One

Do you have a "tragic flaw"? What is the one aspect of your personality that always gets you into trouble? Write a brief scenario in which a "tragic flaw" leads to someone's downfall or failure in life.

The Comic Difference

There are certain aspects that we associate with tragedy and comedy. But perhaps the most important distinction between comedy and tragedy is where the story begins and where it ends.

In traditional tragedy, the main character starts out in a very enviable position. He is powerful, respected, on the rise. Gradually, his prosperity crumbles until at the end of the play the audience witnesses his downfall, and in some cases, his death.

In comedy the main character or characters start out with a mass of problems and complications. Frequently a character's anguish is caused by love. The earliest Greek comedies usually presented a young couple in love who were kept apart by parental disapproval. After a long series of tricks and incredible plot twists, the couple was eventually united in marriage and the disagreeable parents became happy with the match. In fact, you may hear references to the "dance of comedy," based on the idea that at the end of the comic play everyone is joyously paired off.

In its strictest sense *comedy* refers to any piece of literature that has a happy ending. You could hardly view Dante's *The Divine Comedy,* which deals with the author's three-day journey through Hell, Purgatory, and Heaven as a laughfest, but it does meet the criterion of a happy ending. Dante escapes the horrors of Hell and sees the glory of Heaven.

But if you look at those grinning and weeping masks again, you see the popular image of tragedy and comedy. Tragedy affects the heart, the emotions. It has the ability to make you identify so strongly with the main character that you weep at his downfall. You experience what Aristotle referred to as catharsis, the cleansing effect of good tragedy.

Comedy affects the head. Whether comedy depends upon broad physical humor or more subtle verbal cues, you must interpret it before you laugh. There is also an element of emotional superiority present in comedy. You can laugh at the characters because you know you would never find yourself in such a ridiculous predicament, and if you did, you would certainly know how to resolve the problem.

Still, comedy and tragedy are closely linked. One old theory holds that if *someone else* slips on a banana peel, it is comic; if *you* slip on that same peel, it is tragic.

Within the vast spectrum of theatre from pure tragedy to comedy there are other labels that may be used to help differentiate some of the styles.

Types of Drama

Realism, as mentioned in Chapter 1, refers to literature that attempts to portray life as it actually is. Often realism in theatre is explained by the *fourth-wall* concept. As the audience of a realistic drama, you feel as though you have the power to watch life unfold through an invisible fourth wall.

Some writers take this concept a step further to *naturalism.* Although naturalism is an extreme degree of realism, there are differences. The writer of realism may compress events, modify dialogue, and fine-tune characters to give the illusion of reality. The naturalistic writer wants to present dialogue and events exactly as they would occur. But, since most lives plod along at a tedious pace, and most conversations do not reveal profound ideas that present major resolutions, naturalistic plays are sometimes talky and slow moving.

This is certainly not the case with *melodrama,* a general term that may refer to any literature in which the emphasis is on heightened, larger-than-life events. Since there is so much emphasis on events, the characters are often *flat* or one-dimensional. The villain is totally evil. The hero always acts in a noble manner. The heroine never stumbles from virtue.

Types of Comedy

Comedy comes in many subcategories. Exaggeration is the key to many types, such as *high comedy,* in which the emphasis is on intellectual appeal. Often there are intricate puns, wordplay, or fancy language, which appeal to the ear of the audience. Characters, usually of the upper class, are very stiff and artificial, doggedly preserving the manners and behaviors expected of them by society. The high comedy, often comedy of manners, was popular at various times in history. Often these plays were parodies of the overblown, artificial periods in which they were written.

Satire is comedy with a bite. It is directly descended from the earliest writer of comedy, Aristophanes. Satire exaggerates the vices of characters and their society and ridicules events and ideas in an attempt to change some aspect of society, or at least the audience's attitude toward the problem.

Another exaggerated and easily identifiable form of comedy is *farce*. Farce depends upon rapid pacing and extremely broad physical comedy. The characters are seldom *round characters* (well-developed, complex characters who change throughout the play) because they are mere pawns in a ridiculously complicated, unrealistic plot.

The epitome of unrealistic theatre is the *fantasy*. The plot of a fantasy is outside the realm of possibility because the characters and setting are often other-worldly, such as those Alice encounters on her journey through Wonderland.

These distinctions may be helpful in labeling types of drama, but remember that many plays combine elements of these and other types.

Activity Two

What is your favorite TV show? What category do you think it falls into? Cite examples of plot, characterization, and dialogue that prove this.

Activity Three

As a class or in small groups, try to come up with titles of plays, movies, or television shows that typify each category defined.

Presentational and Representational Styles

In addition to the labels already mentioned, the historical period of a play is an important factor in determining how broad the physical action should be, how conversational the actors' tone of voice should be, and how the actors relate to the audience.

These distinctions also contribute to what Alexander Bakshy labeled as *presentational* and *representational* styles.

Most contemporary theatre—with the possible exception of musical comedy, which is very audience conscious—is representational. A production that is representational attempts to realistically represent the world of the play. In representational theatre, the audience technically does not exist, or at least exists outside the realm of the play. In a representational play, an actor's visible awareness of the audience can be a big distraction. Once he or she begins to play to that audience (ham it up) or allows the audience to break his or her concentration, the world so carefully constructed on the stage is destroyed.

Presentational styles of production are those in which the actor is aware of the presence of the audience. The lines and speeches are more declamation than conversation. The actor's body position is more open, often almost full front. The presentational style is common in traditional tragedy and melodrama. In a presentational comedy, the actors may actually address the spectators and play to audience response.

Presentational styles may seem awkward and dated to the modern theatregoer, yet even the conventional, representational styles of theatre make use of certain presentational techniques in dialogue. These include the monologue, soliloquy, and aside.

The *monologue* refers to a long speech in which a character directly addresses another character or characters on stage. In real-life conversations you seldom have the luxury of speaking uninterrupted for two or three minutes. There are questions, disagreements—dialogue. But in drama an actor often has the time to make a point while others listen in rapt attention. Look at the following monologue from *Julius Caesar*. Mark Antony is, on the surface, there to eulogize the recently murdered Caesar. But there are political undertones. Within this brief speech, he must convince the crowd that Caesar was unlawfully murdered and that they should turn against the conspirators with whom they had sided only moments before after hearing Brutus speak about the dangers of Caesar's ambition. Notice how Antony sways the crowd with his emphasis on the honor of Brutus and the other conspirators. The speech addresses the crowd at the forum, but it reveals to the audience much about the character of Mark Antony and foreshadows what is to come.

> Friends, Romans, countrymen, lend me your ears;
> I come to bury Caesar, not to praise him.
> The evil that men do lives after them,
> The good is oft interred with their bones;
> So let it be with Caesar. The noble Brutus
> Hath told you Caesar was ambitious.
> If it were so, it was a grievous fault,
> And grievously hath Caesar answered it.
> Here, under leave of Brutus and the rest
> (For Brutus is an honorable man
> So are they all honorable men),
> Come I to speak in Caesar's funeral.
> He was my friend, faithful and just to me;
> But Brutus says he was ambitious,
> And Brutus is an honorable man.
> He hath brought many captives home to Rome,
> Whose ransoms did the general coffers fill;
> Did this in Caesar seem ambitious?
> When that the poor have cried, Caesar hath wept;
> Ambition should be made of sterner stuff.
> Yet Brutus says he was ambitious;
> And Brutus is an honorable man.
> You all did see that on the Lupercal
> I thrice presented him a kingly crown,
> Which he did thrice refuse. Was this ambition?
> Yet Brutus says he was ambitious;
> And sure he is an honorable man.
> I speak not to disprove what Brutus spoke,
> But here I am to speak what I do know.
> What cause withholds you then to mourn for him?
> O judgment, thou art fled to brutish beasts,
> And men have lost their reason! Bear with me;
> My heart is in the coffin there with Caesar,
> And I must pause till it come back to me.

A *soliloquy* is a speech made by an actor who is alone on stage. It is entirely for the benefit of the audience. Although many people talk to themselves from time to time, the soliloquy seems very contrived until you examine its real purpose. Unlike a novelist, the dramatist does not have any way to make the audience privy to a character's inner thoughts. Everything must be expressed in dialogue or stage directions. The soliloquy allows the character to speak these ideas aloud, and you are allowed to overhear. One of the most famous soliloquies is the following from *Hamlet*. In this speech we see the suicidal depth of Hamlet's despair over the death of his father and his mother's hasty remarriage to his uncle. It is necessary to understand this despair to understand Hamlet's later actions.

> To be or not to be: that is the question.
> Whether 'tis nobler in the mind to suffer
> The slings and arrows of outrageous fortune,
> Or to take arms against a sea of troubles,
> And by opposing end them. To die; to sleep;
> No more; and by a sleep to say we end
> The heart-ache and the thousand natural shocks
> That flesh is heir to. 'Tis a consummation
> Devoutly to be wish'd. To die; to sleep;—
> To sleep? Perchance to dream! Ay, there's the rub
> For in that sleep of death what dreams may come,
> When we have shuffl'd off this mortal coil,
> Must give us pause. There's the respect
> That makes calamity of so long life.
> For who would bear the whips and scorns of time,
> The oppressor's wrong, the proud man's contumely,
> The pangs of dispriz'd love, the law's delay,
> The insolence of office, and the spurns
> That patient merit of the unworthy takes,
> When he himself might his quietus make
> With a bare bodkin? Who would fardels bear,
> To grunt and sweat under a weary life,
> But that the dread of something after death,
> The undiscover'd country from whose bourn
> No traveller returns, puzzles the will
> And makes us rather bear those ills we have
> Than fly to others that we know not of?
> Thus conscience does make cowards of us all;
> And thus the native hue of resolution
> Is sicklied o'er with the pale cast of thought,
> And enterprises of great pith and moment
> With this regard their currents turn awry,
> And lose the name of action.

Finally there is the *aside*, where an actor speaks so that the audience can hear but supposedly the other characters on stage can not. This convention was most heavily utilized in melodrama, where the villain leaned out to the audience to reveal his dastardly plans for the unsuspecting hero. Other uses of the aside may not be so obvious, but they are just as effective. Often a character reveals his or her true thoughts to the audience while playing a very different game on stage. In the following scene from Molière's *The Miser*, the asides point out a misunderstanding between Harpagon and Valere over the phrase "stolen treasure." Harpagon thinks Valere has stolen his money box. Valere thinks Harpagon has discovered his plan to elope with the old man's daughter.

HARPAGON: Come here! Come and confess to the foulest, most dastardly crime that was ever committed.

VALERE: What can I do for you, sir?

HARPAGON: What, you scoundrel! Don't you blush for your crime?

VALERE: What crime are you talking about?

HARPAGON: What crime am I talking about! You infamous wretch! As if you don't know very well what I'm talking about. It's no use your trying to hide it. The secret is out. I've just heard the whole story. To think of your taking advantage of my kindness and getting yourself into my household on purpose to betray me and play a trick like this on me.

VALERE: Well, sir, since you know all about it I won't attempt to excuse or deny it. . . . I have been meaning to speak to you about it. I was waiting for a favourable opportunity, but since things have turned out as they have I can only ask you not to be angry, but be good enough to hear what I have to say in justification.

HARPAGON: And what sort of justification can you give, you scoundrelly thief?

VALERE: Ah sir, I hardly deserve epithets of that kind. It is true that I have put myself in the wrong with you, but, after all, my fault is a pardonable one.

HARPAGON: Pardonable! A stab in the back! A mortal injury!

VALERE: Please don't be angry. When you have heard what I have to say, you'll see that there is less harm done than you think.

HARPAGON: Less harm done than I think. My very heart's blood, you scoundrel!

VALERE: On a question of blood, sir, you haven't done badly. My rank is such that I shall not disgrace your blood and there's nothing in all this that I can't make amends for.

HARPAGON: And that's exactly what I intend that you shall do—you shall return what you've stolen from me.

VALERE: Your honour shall be fully satisfied, sir.

HARPAGON: There's no question of honour! Tell me, what on earth led you to do such a thing?

VALERE: Do you really need ask?

HARPAGON: Of course I need ask.

VALERE: It was that little god who is always forgiven, whatever he makes people do. Love, I mean.

HARPAGON: Love!

VALERE: Of course.

HARPAGON: A pretty sort of love! Upon my word! Love of my gold pieces.

VALERE: No, sir, it was not your wealth that tempted me, not in the least. That's not what dazzled me! Let me assure you I have no aspirations whatever where your wealth is concerned, provided you let me keep the one treasure I already possess.

HARPAGON: No, indeed! By all the devils in Hell! You shan't keep it. The impudence! Wanting to keep what he's stolen.

VALERE: Do you really call it stealing?

HARPAGON: Do I really call it stealing? A treasure like that?

VALERE: Yes, a treasure indeed, and beyond question the most precious you have, but not lost to you in becoming mine. On my bended knees I beg you to accord me this most cherished of treasures. Surely you can't refuse your consent.

HARPAGON: I'll do nothing of the sort. What on earth are you talking about?

VALERE: We are promised to each other and sworn never to be parted.

HARPAGON: A wonderful promise! A remarkable compact, I must say!

VALERE: Yes, we are bound to one another forever.

HARPAGON: I'll put a stop to that, I promise you.

VALERE: Death alone shall part us.

HARPAGON: He must have my money on the brain!

VALERE: I've already told you, sir, I was not moved to do what I have done by material considerations. My motive was not what you think, but a far nobler one.

HARPAGON: He'll be telling me next that it's sheer Christian charity set him wanting my money. But I'll see to that, and the law shall give me satisfaction on you, you impudent scoundrel.

VALERE: Do as you please. I am resigned to bear whatever violence you may resort to, but I do ask you to believe that if any fault has been committed, I alone am guilty. Your daughter is in no way to blame.

HARPAGON: I should think not, indeed! It would be a queer thing if my daughter were involved in a crime like this. But I want to be seeing you make restoration. Where's the hiding place?

VALERE: There's no question of restoration or of hiding place since we have not left the house.

HARPAGON: (aside) Oh, my treasure! (to Valere) Not left the house, you say?

VALERE: No sir.

HARPAGON: Now tell me—you haven't been tampering—

VALERE: Never! There you wrong both of us. My love is pure and honourable, and though I am so deeply in love—

HARPAGON: (aside) Deeply in love—with my cash box?

VALERE: I would die sooner than harbour a single thought unworthy of one so kind and modest as—

HARPAGON: (aside) Modest—my cash box?

VALERE:	I have asked nothing more than the pleasure of feasting my eyes upon her. Nothing base or unworthy has ever profaned the love which her beauty inspires in me.
HARPAGON:	(*aside*) Beauty—my cash box? You might think he was a lover talking of his mistress.
VALERE:	Dame Claude knows the truth of the matter, sir. She can bear witness.
HARPAGON:	Ha, so my servant is in the plot, is she?
VALERE:	Yes, sir, she was a witness to our vows. Once she found that my intentions were honourable, she helped me to persuade your daughter to give me her promise and accept mine in return.
HARPAGON:	(*aside*) Fear of justice must have turned his brain! (*to Valere*) What has my daughter to do with it?
VALERE:	I am just saying, sir, that I had the greatest difficulty in persuading her to accept my advances.
HARPAGON:	Accept your advances? Who?
VALERE:	Why it was not until yesterday that she gave me her promise to marry me.
HARPAGON:	My daughter has given her promise to marry you?
VALERE:	Yes, sir—as I gave her mine in return.
HARPAGON:	Heavens! Another disaster!

Even though you are probably much more familiar with the representational style used in TV and movies, many directors use snatches of the presentational. For instance, take note of Ferris Bueller's (played by Matthew Broderick) dead-on comments to the camera in John Hughes' 1986 film *Ferris Bueller's Day Off*. Pure presentational theatre.

Conflict

Labels and definitions help us delineate certain types of drama, but these are very flexible lines, always yielding to overlapping and newly emerging forms of theatre. But no matter what form it takes, all drama is based on *conflict*. There has to be some problem to be resolved, whether it is individual vs. individual, individual vs. nature, individual vs. society, individual vs. himself. Once the playwright decides on the nature of the conflict, he or she must decide on the framework within which that conflict will build.

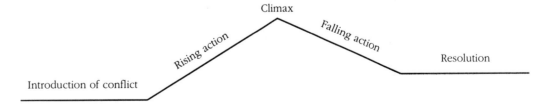

Figure 2.1
Structure of conflict

If you look at the diagram for the structure of conflict, you will realize that it is somewhat like climbing a mountain, or riding a roller coaster. The conflict is introduced early on; then the build begins. There may be several crags and dips along the way, but there is the top-most part, the *climax,* where the action irrevocably turns and all that is left is the resolution. Obviously, the length of the play is the main factor for determining where the climax, the highest point of the action, will occur.

The ancient tragedies were tightly structured with choral odes, parade and exodus scenes, and other specialized segments interspersed between the scenes. Still, probably because the individual tragedies were parts of a trilogy often performed together, each ran about the length of a modern one-act.

A one-act play is the literary equivalent of a short story. It can be digested in one sitting, under an hour, usually half that. This short form, which focuses on a limited time frame and limited number of characters, seems eternally popular. But many playwrights needed a longer format to bring their conflicts to a satisfactory resolution. The specific structure varied at different times in the history of the theatre.

Through the Renaissance, the standard full-length play ran five acts. Molière and Shakespeare unerringly followed the format. Later, the realistic dramatists favored a four-act structure. Then the standard became three acts. Today, some plays are in three acts but most have gone to a two-act structure. Typical of our rushed society, a modern audience is willing to sit for a shorter period of time, with only one break in the action. Often, Shakespeare's or Ibsen's carefully crafted structure is modified to fit our desire for a hurried theatrical experience. Still, this compressed form can work if the buildup of the conflict and its ultimate resolution are believable. Knowing how to pace the introduction, rising action, and resolution of the conflict is a skill more important to the dramatist than any other writer. The audience cannot lay aside the novel that begins to drag and resume the story at a later time, or skip pages to get to the good parts. The audience is there and must be satisfied with the pacing of the action as it occurs. Nothing else can substitute for the well-crafted script.

No matter how you label it, no matter what structure the playwright uses to reach the final resolution, everything on stage grows from the words on paper, the script. Shakespeare was right. "The play's the thing."

3 Setting the Scene

Stages, Sets, Lighting, and Props

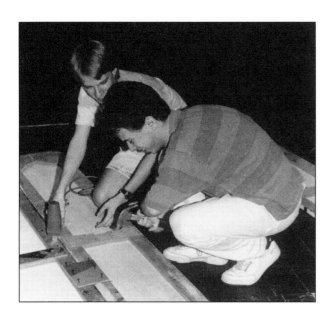

Activity One

Read the following scene carefully.

#1: Oh.

#2: Yes.

#1: Why are you doing this?

#2: It's the best thing.

#1: You can't mean it.

#2: No, I'm serious.

#1: Please.

#2: What . . .

#1: What does this mean?

#2: Nothing.

#1: Listen—

#2: No.

#1: So different . . .

#2: Not really.

#1: Oh.

#2: You're right.

#1: Forget it.

#2: What?

#1: Go on.

#2: I will.

When you look at the format of any published play, you will note the first thing provided is a cast list, often with a brief description of each character. Next, there is a description of the setting—the time and place. Very often there is a detailed description of the scene. Sometimes you may be tempted to skip straight to the dialogue because you think these elements are less important. Think again. What is happening? Who are these characters labeled #1 and #2.

It is easy to assume that a play is just a series of lines of dialogue. But as the previous exercise (first conceived by Wandalie Henshaw as an exercise for directing) shows, without context, there can be many different interpretations of lines. Setting is the context for the characters and their words and actions. Just as a real person is the product of his or her environment, a character is the product of his or her setting.

Keep in mind that setting refers to both time and place. The sly slave in a comedy by Plautus is at a much greater risk and must spin his wild schemes in much greater secrecy than the household servant in a comedy by Molière because the head of the household had much more power over his servants in ancient Rome than in seventeenth-century France.

Even societies existing in the same time frame can be quite different. A simple love story revolving around two teenagers might be quite different in a city of two million people compared to a small town of three thousand. What differences in these stories come to your mind?

Aside from just the date and place of the action, the playwright also must establish what is referred to as the *cultural milieu*—the norms, values, ideals, and problems of that particular society.

But even this is not enough. Within even the smallest town, there are specific social classes, ethnic groups, and cultural strata. Even within these subdivisions there are individual tastes and eccentricities that stamp a character's space as his or her own.

Activity Two

Imagine that you are going to write an autobiographical play. The setting might be your living room, bedroom, a classroom, or another place where you spend time. What details might you include to give the audience a specific sense of setting?

Once again, the playwright is working with a different set of rules than other writers. The novelist may give page after page of description to set the scene and may change scenes in every chapter.

The playwright may give italicized stage directions that help the *reader* visualize the setting, but when the play is transported to its ultimate form, when it is performed before an audience, that written description is lost. It now rests with the set designer to reproduce those impressions visually so that as the lights "go up," the audience is transported to the appropriate time and place. Since this "world" of the play must be constructed concretely, the playwright usually cannot change setting as often as the novelist; scene changes must be kept to a minimum.

There are several ways in which the world of the play may be constructed. Which method is used ultimately depends on the staging area, the flexibility required if more than one setting is called for, the budget of the production, and the skill of the crew.

Types of Stages

A play can be produced almost anywhere. The ancient Greeks used large amphitheatres. The seventeenth-century French converted tennis courts. You may have seen performances in large theatres, school auditoriums, or tiny studio theatres.

In any theatre there is a distinction between the *house* (where the audience sits) and the *stage* (where the actors perform). Most stages are one of three types: *arena, thrust,* or *proscenium.* They are categorized according to where the audience sits in relation to the stage.

Arena staging is often referred to as theatre-in-the-round. The stage is in the center and the audience sits on all four sides. Because the audience is all around, arena staging does not allow for massive, elaborate sets that block the view of some part of the audience.

Theoretically, there are no bad seats in an arena setting because the action moves all over the stage; this presents a special set of challenges for the actor and director. Although you may think of "arena" as indicating a huge facility, many small theatres utilize the arena concept because it provides a very intimate setting.

The *thrust* stage is really a modified arena stage. The stage juts or "thrusts" out into the audience so that audience sits on three sides. The thrust stage provides much of the intimacy of the arena stage but allows for backstage area and more scenery. It also, however, provides some special difficulties in keeping the sight lines clear for the entire audience.

The most common type of stage in high school auditoriums is the *proscenium.* With a proscenium stage, the audience sits in front of the stage and looks directly at the action. The proscenium is often compared to a picture frame.

Obviously, this was the favorite of those who advocated the fourth-wall concept of realism. With proscenium staging, it is possible to construct an elaborate set that actually reproduces the inside of a home.

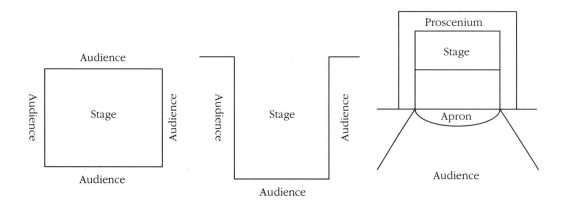

Figure 3.1
Arena stage

Figure 3.2
Thrust stage

Figure 3.3
Proscenium stage

Activity Three

Using the guidelines given for identifying the three types of stages, give examples of each that you are familiar with. What play or event did you attend there? What impressions do you have of that type of staging?

If you look at a proscenium stage, it is possible to further subdivide the acting space into nine areas.

Up Right	Up Center	Up Left
Right Center	Center	Left Center
Down Right	Down Center	Down Left

Audience

Figure 3.4
The nine areas of the proscenium stage

There is no question about the derivation of *center stage,* but the others may take some explanation. The front of the stage is downstage, the back of the stage is upstage. The terms come directly from the ancient Greek theatres where the stage was raked or angled in such a way that the front of the stage was literally lower (*downstage*) and the back was higher (*upstage*).

Since downstage is obviously the stronger position for an actor, you might wonder about the term "upstaging." Look at that diagram again. If two actors are conversing on stage and one steps slightly upstage, what happens? The other must turn away from the audience to face him or her. The first actor has drawn the audience's focus entirely, and the second actor has been upstaged.

Finally, the labels stage right and stage left seem to be reversed. Remember that the actor is facing the audience. The actor's right is the audience's left. On stage, right and left are always determined by the actor's right and left.

Types of Sets

Once you are familiar with the type of stage you are working with, you may begin thinking about the specific acting area created for the play, the set. Whether you decide to work with backdrops, set pieces, or a full set will depend upon the amount of time, money, and skill you have to devote to the scenery.

The set description given in the script is often based upon elaborate professional production standards. Clearly you will not have the turntable sets or rising platforms available to many Broadway productions. You must decide how the design can be modified to fit your stage, your budget, and your building skills.

The most elaborate form of production is a full set with flats. *Flats,* are wooden frameworks, which are covered on one side with tightly stretched muslin. They are of varying sizes (typically around four or five feet wide by ten feet high). As you will see from the diagram, these frameworks must be well constructed because all the individual flats eventually will be hinged or lashed together to form a background that is then painted to look like a living room, a city street, and so on.

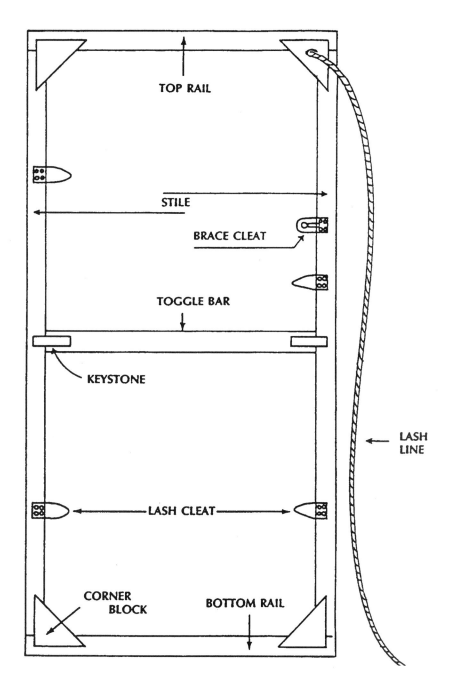

Figure 3.5
Parts of a flat

A full set with flats provides the most realistic set, and the flats may be repainted and used again and again, but this process is expensive and time consuming. It requires considerable construction skill, and it can only be accomplished in an auditorium where you have the space and facilities for constructing flats and storing them between productions.

If the full-set concept seems overwhelming, there are other ways to create the illusion of a different time and place. Some productions use with great success painted backdrops suspended from the backstage overhead rail system.

Probably the easiest way to produce the illusion of setting is with set pieces. *Set pieces* consist of furniture or large stationary pieces that suggest the play's environment. Set pieces are essential for arena staging but can be used just as effectively on a proscenium stage. A settee upholstered in velvet, an antique table, a hurricane lamp and a window frame hung with delicate lace curtains can go a long way toward suggesting a Victorian living room.

This simplified form of production has a long history in theatre. The ancient Greek and Elizabethan theatres used almost no sets. In fact, Elizabethan sets were so notoriously sparse that often when Shakespeare's characters entered, there was some subtle line references that established the time and place. A more sparse set puts emphasis on the actors and on the play itself, which can be an advantage.

Activity Four

Choose a play from the library. Read the description of the set as it is given in the script. Detail how you would modify this for a less elaborate setting.

Lighting

When you attend the theatre, you talk about going to *see* a play. That is the first and foremost function of lighting; it allows you to see the action on stage.

In the days before electric lights, plays were performed in open-air theatres during daylight hours. The first indoor theatres were illuminated by candles along the lower edge of the stage (limelight) or gas lamps above or behind the actors.

Lighting has come a long way since then, and a good lighting designer, in addition to making the play visible, helps create the mood of the play and may contribute any special effects called for.

There are several lighting terms that you should be familiar with. *House lights* refer to those fixtures that light the audience portion of the theatre. When you walk into a theatre before a performance, the house lights are on. When the house lights begin to dim, it is your cue that you are about to be transported to the world of the play. When the house lights come back on at intermission, you know that world of the play has been temporarily suspended and you are free to talk to your friends or get up and move about the theatre.

But what about the lights that illuminate the stage area itself? There are several different types of stage lighting. *Footlights* are probably the oldest form of electric stage lights. Footlights are a strip of lights that runs along the downstage area at floor level. Usually they are a combination of white, blue, and red lights. Many older auditoriums and theatres are equipped with footlights; however, because they throw uneven, shadowy light, footlights are seldom used today, except as an accessory to other types of lighting.

Most backstage areas are equipped with *flood lights*. These large lights are convenient to illuminate backstage work areas, but they are seldom used for lighting the stage during a performance because such lighting cannot be focused easily and may spill over the entire area.

Another type of lighting device is the *follow spotlight* (see Figure 3.6). As the name implies, the follow spot usually follows a performer across the stage during a musical number or an important speech. However, it may be left in a fixed position to highlight a certain area of the stage.

Figure 3.6
Follow spotlight

Most lighting plots depend upon a number of smaller, fixed spotlights. These may include the types pictured in Figure 3.7.

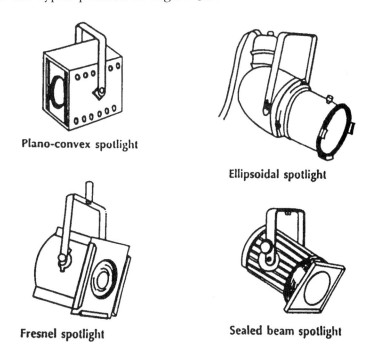

Plano-convex spotlight

Ellipsoidal spotlight

Fresnel spotlight

Sealed beam spotlight

Figure 3.7
Four types of spotlights

All of these can be focused to illuminate the entire stage or highlight certain areas. These lighting instruments may be suspended from the stage ceiling, the balcony rails or, as is currently popular with concerts and traveling shows, lighting trees.

Because intense stage lighting can "wash out" the actors on stage, lights are often treated with gels. *Gels* are transparent, tinted-plastic sheets inserted in front of the lamps to counteract the harshness of clear white light. Lights may be gelled to warm actors' skin tones, make the sky blue, or contribute to special effects.

All lighting instruments should be connected to some kind of dimming mechanism. Unless the director wants the dramatic effect of a quick blackout, no audience likes to be jarred in and out of the realm of the play with the flick of a switch. Besides allowing the audience to ease in and out of the world on stage, dimmers can effectively simulate sunrises, sunsets, and so forth.

As with the set itself, lighting can be simple or complex depending on the needs and budget of your particular production.

Props

Although lighting and setting can be minimized, most productions make full use of properties, or props. *Props* are the small, portable items that are either set on the stage or carried by the actors. Like the set and set pieces, they do a great deal to establish time and place. The tragic illusion of the poisoning in the last act of *Hamlet* is irrevocably broken if Gertrude drinks from a plastic cup. With the many references to the setting of the 1930s in *You Can't Take It With You,* the audience will be disturbed if Penny sits down to work at an electric typewriter.

You probably will not be able to use antiques and authentic period pieces for every prop, but the audience must believe the illusion of a particular time and place, and nothing breaks that illusion more quickly than an obvious *anachronism,* something out of place by time.

Props reveal a lot about their owners, too. If a character is hanging a painting in his new apartment, is it an abstract print, a delicate watercolor, or Elvis on velvet? If a character is carrying a purse, is it a neat clutch, a handy shoulder bag, or a bottomless tote?

Props are also important in advancing the plot. If the elderly ladies in *Arsenic and Old Lace* are poisoning guests with tea, the tea set must be on stage. If Lady Macbeth's ambition is fueled by reading about her husband's encounter with the three weird sisters, the letter must be in her hand. If Desdemona is betrayed to Othello by a stolen handkerchief, the audience must be able to follow that prop. These details are important; someone needs to make sure the props are in place.

Since props are so important to the production, they must be chosen with care. The head of the prop crew, the *property manager,* must begin assembling props, or at least substitute props, as soon as possible. You may not want to use the bone china tea set for a month of rehearsals, but actors need to start practicing picking up and getting rid of props that don't just materialize from or dissolve into thin air.

If you are in charge of props, your first step may be to check the prop room, usually an odd assemblage of leftovers from previous shows. After combing through this repository, you must decide whether the remaining props you need will have to be borrowed, bought, or constructed.

If you decide to construct, remember that you have the advantage of distance. The audience will not be near enough to the stage for close scrutiny, but the prop must look real from the house and it must hold up through rehearsals and performance. Some props, such as a disturbing letter that gets crumpled and tossed aside, must be redone every night.

Activity Five

Using the same play you chose for scene design, make a list of all props called for in the play. Label each item *Have, Borrow, Buy,* or *Construct.* If you were to look at this as a "scavenger hunt" list, where would you borrow the items you have listed? How would you construct the items listed?

Once you have assembled all the props needed for the show, you must determine which are *set props* and which are *hand props.* The set props are the ones placed on the set before the play or during a scene change. It is the prop crew's responsibility to make sure these things are set correctly each night.

Hand props are carried onto the stage by the actor, but they must be precisely set on a backstage prop table. If there are a large number of hand props, the prop table should be set for each act. Every prop should be in the same place on the prop table each night and returned to that spot after it is used.

No matter how fascinating they are, no one should be allowed to play with the props. These items should not be handled by anyone except the crew and those actors who need to use them on stage.

Attention to details of setting allows the audience to be transported to that other time and place. True, setting is an illusion, but any backstage crew knows how much hard labor goes into that illusion.

4 Characterization Through Costumes and Makeup

Why Do You Dress Me in Borrowed Robes?—Macbeth

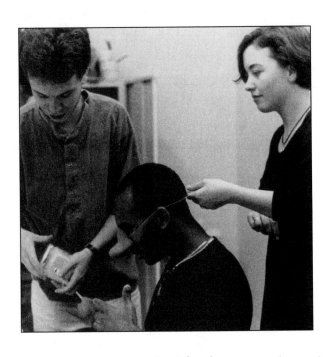

Go back to your favorite childhood game of "let's pretend." Was it a society tea party? Or a cowboy on the range? How did costuming figure into these play activities?

Do you remember your favorite Halloween or dance recital costume? Maybe your Little League uniform? What made it so special? How did you feel when you put it on?

There is something innately tempting about temporarily wanting to take on another identity. Theatre is a more sophisticated form of this identity assumption performed for an audience. Costuming helps an actor get into character, but more importantly, it gives the audience clues about the character and his or her society.

Although all shows require *costumes* (the clothes that the actors wear on stage), some shows are characterized as straight shows rather than full-costume shows.

Straight shows are plays whose setting is in the present. There is nothing odd or exotic about the way the characters dress. For this type of play, actors may go to their own closets or borrow from friends or family members clothing that seems right for the character. However, just because clothing for characters in a straight play may be more easily accessible, costuming is not any less important.

Activity One

Costume the following characters for a play. Tell what they look like and what they are wearing.

1. A high school English teacher
2. A college physics professor

3. A private detective

4. A cocktail waitress

5. A society matron

6. A former pro football player

7. A used-car salesperson

8. An attorney

9. A homemaker

10. A night clerk at a convenience store

11. A high school prom queen

12. A computer whiz

Now compare your descriptions for the above characters. You may find some shocking similarities in these characters because it is likely that you have costumed stereotypes. *Stereotyping* categorizes all people who belong to a particular group by broad generalizations, and assumes that they share the same physical and emotional characteristics.

Types of Characters

These stereotypes or *stock characters* have a long history in theatre. Many characters such as the pompous scholar, the doddering old man, the crafty servant, or the young couple in love can be found in ancient Greek and Roman comedy.

These characters and a few others were thoroughly entrenched in the commedia del l'arte. Actors in these traveling commedia troupes specialized in one or two characters, which they played throughout their lifetimes. So important was the audience's instant identification of these character types that the actors were costumed for immediate recognition.

One stock type that we still recognize is Harlequin, the commedia character who helped pace the action with somersaults, juggling, and gymnastics. Harlequin was the character in the brightly colored diamond-patched tunic, whom we associate with a medieval jester or fool. Another easily recognizable character is the learned doctor or the pompous scholar, clad all in flowing black, except for his white collar and cuffs. If you think this costume is no longer relevant, think how you will be attired at graduation to show that you have entered the realms of the learned.

So, while stereotypes may be fine for *flat* or one-dimensional characters, most contemporary playwrights work with *round* or more complex characters. They may find more interest in a physics professor who aspires to be a stand-up comic or a cocktail waitress who also attends law school.

Activity Two

Go back and choose one of those flat characters from Activity 1 and develop a round character. What makes that character unique? Does this make a difference in how you costume that character?

Of course it is the actor's responsibility to fully develop a character, but just as a person dresses to project a certain image, costuming helps to project a character's image. Before an actor ever utters a line, the first impression a character makes is visual. Costuming can suggest age, occupation, social class, style, personality, and general attitude. Like any visual artist, one of the major factors a costumer relies on is color.

The Significance of Color

Activity Three

What do these color choices seem to reveal about the characters wearing them?

1. A navy suit
2. A red dress
3. A yellow sweater
4. A khaki uniform
5. A pink shirt
6. A purple cape

Color has very strong connotations for us. Some are societal, such as black for mourning and white for a bride; others are personal. A popular trend in the past few years has been "having your colors done," based upon the idea that people can be divided—based upon skin tones, eye and hair color—into seasons: summer, winter, spring, and fall. Whether or not you believe this theory, there is no question that color has an impact. If you doubt this, think about your own wardrobe. Does any one color predominate? What is there about that color that appeals to you? Is there a color that you hate? What negative thing to you associate with that color?

Aside from color, does the character dress for style or comfort? Is she neat or sloppy? Is she rich or poor? Does she dress in a particular way for work and another for leisure? All of these are important considerations.

As in real life, much of a character's individuality is expressed in accessories. Does she wear flashy jewelry, stylish scarves, or prim white gloves? Just as you fairly or unfairly judge people by your visual impression, so do you judge characters. If you accept the old adage that clothes make the person, be doubly assured that they make the character.

The Costume or Period Show

The idea of period costuming is relatively new when compared to the entire history of theatre. The Greeks wore character masks, but most of the costumes were simply long robes. Elizabethan actors wore their everyday clothing. If the Elizabethan actor was playing a king or a priest, he might add a crown or a cross, but that was about the limit of the authenticity.

Today's audience expects a greater attempt at realism. All the elements of costuming as it relates to developing the individual character are still important, but there is something else to be considered. The costumes in a period drama must reflect the period or time frame in which the play is set. Just as anachronisms in props disturb an audience, so do costumes that suggest the wrong era.

Even a decade can make a tremendous difference in style. You have probably looked at (and snickered at) old pictures of your great-aunt in a poodle skirt, your mother in bell-bottoms, or your uncle in a leisure suit. Enjoy the laugh. Someday your children may be doing the same thing to you.

Thanks to fashion magazines and television, it is true that styles change much more rapidly today, but styles did change in earlier centuries. In some eras you could pinpoint an American geographically by how in tune he or she was with Eastern fashion. Similarly, trends that began in one city in Europe sometimes spread throughout the continent.

Often a radical departure in style, such as the 1920s flapper look, was a social as well as a fashion statement. And you will understand the odd combination of pampered life-style and painful vanity when you look at the antebellum Southern belle dresses of *Gone with the Wind*.

So how do you research what turn fashion took in a particular era? Fortunately, there are wonderful costume handbooks and encyclopedias to show you what clothing looked like in various social classes in specific locations and historical periods. It is also helpful to read history and see why these trends in clothing developed. Although clothing expresses an individual's style and a culture's whimsical sense of fashion, there may be practical reasons why certain trends developed. A cowboy's chaps made hours on horseback much more comfortable. Shorter skirts allowed women more freedom of movement. Broad-brimmed hats protected their wearers from the sun.

Activity Four

Choose a play from another time period. Suggestions include *Hamlet, The Crucible, Cyrano de Bergerac, Julius Caesar, A Doll's House, You Can't Take it With You, Antigone, Camelot*. Decide exactly what time period the play covers. Check costume books and other historical sources, then draw or describe in detail three major characters' costumes. Think about what was happening in the society at that time that may have affected clothing styles.

Deciding Whether to Rent or Construct Costumes

For a period drama, few actors will be able to open their closets and pull out appropriate garb. You must now decide whether you will construct or rent costumes for the play. There are several things to consider in this group decision.

Do you have the space and facilities to construct and store costumes? As in constructing scenery, there must be work space for assembling costumes. After all the work you have put in on the project, you will want someplace to store costumes after the production is over.

Do you have the skill in design and construction to create the costumes? Once again you are working with distance. The audience may not notice a slightly crooked hem or the fact that the jeweled trim has been hot-glued to a tunic, but it may be very hard to even come close to reproducing some of the elaborate gowns and waistcoats for the characters in a Molière comedy.

Finally, will you be able to use the costumes again? Renting and constructing are both expensive propositions. If you are planning on a yearly Shakespeare festival, constructing costumes for *Hamlet* makes sense. But, if you are sure this is a one-time foray into Elizabethan drama, renting is probably the best option.

Sometimes the most sensible idea is a combination of the two strategies: constructing the simple costumes and renting the more complicated ones. There are numerous costume houses that have in stock costumes from a variety of plays and time periods. All they need are the play's title, the dates of production, and the actors' measurements. Constructing and renting are both viable options depending on whether you want to build your costume wardrobe for future productions or have more time to emphasize other aspects of the production at hand.

The most important thing about period costumes is that the actors start working, as soon as possible, in rehearsal costumes that simulate the particular styles of the period. If an actress will be wearing a long skirt with a hoop petticoat or high heels, she will move very differently than she does when rehearsing in sneakers and sweats. If an actor is going to feel uncomfortable in tights and a tunic, don't let him wait till final dress rehearsal to get accustomed to the costume. Remember, the audience must believe that these costumes are the character's real clothing.

Stage Makeup

Closely tied to costuming as one of the external aspects of character development is makeup. Makeup does two things; it counteracts lighting and it suggests character.

Every actor will be wearing some sort of makeup. It evens out skin tone and provides more depth of color in the harsh glare of stage lighting. The base makeup is most often greasepaint or pancake. *Greasepaint* comes in a tube and is dotted on the skin and then blended onto the face with damp fingers. *Pancake* base comes in a flat, round cake. It is applied with a wet sponge. Greasepaint is heavier and provides more total coverage, but pancake looks more natural up close. One or the other is used before applying any rouge, eye makeup, lip color, or character definition, such as age lines.

Most character makeup plots will require more than just a base. It may be as simple as adding eyeliner or cheek color to give the face definition. It may be something more specific to the character. In many school productions, since all of the actors fall into the same age range, it is necessary to do age makeup on some characters.

The word in age makeup is subtlety. Remember, you are creating the illusion of an elderly character, not reminding the audience that you are a teen-ager playing an old person. Study your face carefully; it is the only canvas on which you can believably create this illusion. Are you going to have dark circles when you are older? Smile and frown intently while looking into the mirror. Where are the natural creases these grimaces leave? These are the "lines" you have to work with. If the age lines you draw on your face do not match these natural lines, you will have a distorted double image every time your facial expression changes.

With a soft brush dipped in greasestick (just what the name implies, greasepaint in a soft stick) or thin brown pencil, draw lines that exactly lie in the creases of your smile and frown lines. You may then highlight them (using a greasestick lighter than the skin tone) on either side of the dark line. Blend carefully in the direction of the lines, and powder the entire face, pressing powder onto the face, then brushing away the excess. This sets the makeup thoroughly. Later it must be removed with tissues and heavy cold cream.

Although age makeup is the most common specialized makeup, it is certainly not the only challenge to the makeup artist.

Activity Five

Decide how you would design makeup for one of the following characters. Or if you have access to stage cosmetics, actually apply the makeup.

1. An elderly man or woman
2. One of the witches from Shakespeare's *Macbeth*
3. The Lion from George Bernard Shaw's *Androcles and the Lion*
4. The March Hare from Lewis Carroll's *Alice's Adventures in Wonderland*
5. Puck from Shakespeare's *A Midsummer Night's Dream*

Makeup also includes hair, meaning the actor's natural hair and any wigs, falls, or constructed beards. Once again, be familiar with the styles of the play's time period.

Take a look through a parent's or old relative's high school yearbooks. Nothing becomes outdated as quickly as trendy hairstyles. Most makeup books and many costume books will also give information on hairstyles.

On rare occasions makeup may include a *prosthesis* or specially constructed appliance. For example, in Rostand's *Cyrano de Bergerac,* Cyrano's nose is the object of much ridicule and many duels. Few actors naturally have a nose outrageous enough to be the centerpiece of a character and must resort to nose putty, a claylike substance that is molded to the actor's nose before the makeup is applied. These special makeup challenges must be well thought out by the makeup designer so that they are comfortable enough not to distract the actor.

As with costuming, there are excellent books on theatrical makeup, but there is no substitute for experimentation. Makeup is one area where you can truly keep trying and revising until you get it right.

5 The Actor's Role

A Method in the Madness—Hamlet

Human beings love to pretend, to assume another persona for some period of time. Acting carries the childhood game of "let's pretend" to a new level of sophistication in that it is thoroughly rehearsed and performed for an audience who should come away entertained, instructed, or in some way changed by the experience.

"Becoming" another human being on stage is a complicated art that requires intense study and practice. Although costuming and makeup help establish character, the actor essentially is working with his or her own personal assets. While a musician is dependent upon his piano or clarinet, an actor is dependent upon voice and body—in short, the actor's instrument.

Interpreting a Role

You may have seen two equally skilled actors play the same role, yet find that you prefer one rendering of the character over the other. You have just seen the value of the actor's interpretation.

Above all else, the actor must be believable to the audience. There are many factors affecting the portrayal of a character.

Character Type

Many actors complain of being typecast. *Typecasting* casts the performer in a particular role because he or she is similar in personality, appearance or demeanor to the character. Most actors love being cast against type because it allows them to challenge themselves and show their versatility.

When looking at character type, there are many physical aspects to be considered, such as age, race, ethnic group, and physical features. Often some of these physical characteristics are essential to the character. Shakespeare's Falstaff is usually portrayed as a man whose great appetites have provided him with great physical girth. As a historical figure, Abraham Lincoln is universally remembered as tall. If an adult is cast in a child's role, it is presumed that he or she will not tower over the grown-up characters on stage.

Many of the actor's physical discrepancies with the character may be overcome by costuming or makeup, but is the final performance worth these cumbersome additions, or is there someone else more suited to the role? Sometimes an actor may just have to accept his or her physical limitations.

Character Development

Since most plays do not so specifically "type" a character, and since many of these discrepancies can be resolved by makeup and wardrobe, there are other aspects to the development of a character which become paramount.

One is the character's background. Where is the character's birthplace? What were the circumstances of his or her upbringing? What is the level of his or her education? What is his or her occupational record? Hobbies? What religious, political, and philosophical beliefs does he or she adhere to?

Many actors in preparation for a role delve so deeply into the character's background that they could write a detailed biography of this fictional character. In order to understand where characters end up, it is important to understand where they come from.

Perhaps even more important than a character's past is the present. In order to successfully portray a character, an actor must have a certain understanding of the character's feelings. This understanding of and ability to relate to a character's feelings is called *empathy*.

Empathy allows an actor to know a character's *motivation,* the reason for his or her words and actions.

Many lines of dialogue and actions seem so appropriate that their motivations are obvious. But what makes Iago destroy the lives of noble Othello and innocent Desdemona? Why does Cyrano not tell Roxanne he wrote Christian's love letters until fifteen years after his rival's death and fifteen minutes before his own? Why does Medea murder her children to take revenge on her husband?

These motivations seem more obscure. These are not everyday actions. An actor, while maybe not agreeing with these actions, must have enough empathy with the character to understand why these choices seem justified in that character's mind and make their occurrence believable to the audience. The history of theatre has spawned several ways of dealing with this problem.

The Greek theatre was ceremonial in style, and most theatre until well past the turn of the century was presentational in style. Because of this, there was not much emphasis on an actor being natural in a role, especially in the portrayal of a larger-than-life tragic figure. The emphasis was on the full, resonant voice and sweeping gestures that could be heard and seen throughout the audience.

Today with movie close-ups and the small-screen intimacy of television, these vocal and physical enlargements would be annoying, even ludicrous.

There are two major schools of acting that may be viewed as valuable to the actor.

Acting—The Technical Method

The so-called technical method really evolved from ancient Greek and Roman oratorical styles. It focused on the idea that there were certain vocal inflections, postures, facial expressions, and gestures that most convincingly conveyed certain emotions. The French Technical Method reached its peak in the eighteenth century. This method, codified and popularized by François Delsarte, on the surface seems to be a cataloging of the worst excesses of melodrama. We snicker at the melodramatic hand-to-the-forehead gesture of despair; but, Delsarte's idea is not entirely without merit.

Activity One

Describe or enact the posture, facial expressions, and gestures you would associate with these situations.

1. A young man at the funeral of a close friend
2. A girl who has just been dumped by her boyfriend
3. The player who scored the winning touchdown in a championship game
4. A young couple in love
5. A woman waiting in the outer office before an important job interview
6. A man being pulled over by the state police for reckless driving
7. A student falsely accused of cheating on a test

There are certain physical characteristics that accompany emotional states. If you don't believe it, how do you know that your best friend had a terrific weekend? Or that your English teacher is in a rotten mood? How do your parents always know when you are guilty of something? Physicalization gives you away every time.

Delsarte's method seems to work from the outside in. The assumption is that by manifesting the outward appearances of an emotion, the actor comes to embody that emotion.

Method Acting

The other major school of acting is Stanislavski's method, often referred to as just "the Method." Constantin Stanislavski developed this idea in his work with the famous Moscow Art Theatre. Through such American disciples as actor/director/teacher Lee Strasberg, the Method has become one of the primary schools of acting studied today.

Stanislavski believed that in order to successfully reproduce an emotion on stage, one must be able to get in touch with a similar emotion in oneself. In other words, *if* you were that character, *if* you were in that situation, how would you react? The successful method actor should make the audience believe that he or she is living the events of the drama, not just playing them on stage. There are numerous books available on method acting, several by Stanislavski himself, which may be helpful in providing further explanation of this system.

Activity Two

What event from your past would you conjure up to help you get in touch with a particular emotion so that you might successfully portray it on stage?

1. Infatuation

2. Fear

3. Anger

4. Grief

5. Confusion

Getting in touch with an empathetic emotion clearly is helpful in portraying a character, but sometimes there is nothing in your past that you can tap into for an emotional conduit. Then you may wish to rely on the technical method.

Although method acting is by far the more widespread system today, most actors adapt from all systems what works best for them on stage.

Activity Three

Choose a contemporary figure—someone who has been in the news—or a figure from history or literature who has committed an act alien to your own moral code. Write a brief profile of this character from the first person point of view. Explain the motivation for your actions. If you were to take on the role of this character, how would this exercise affect your portrayal?

The Dual Nature of Acting

The internal/external nature of acting is only part of the paradox. The actor must be into the role enough that the audience believes he or she is the character. The actor must not break character if something unexpected happens on stage. If someone forgets a line, if the doorbell doesn't ring on cue, if a prop is missing, these problems must be taken care of in character.

Yet as an actor, you cannot be so deeply into the character that you neglect all responsibility for creating the audience's illusion. You must be in the light rather than in the shadows. You must be aware of your body position, so that you do not turn your back to the audience or upstage another actor.

Once again there is the duality of the masks. The actor, for the duration of the play, enters into the illusion of becoming the character. However, he or she is always the actor, always in control of the character. The actor can never let that fictional person become the driving force of the performance.

This tightrope of actor/character and the tenuous illusion on the stage are created by the actor's voice and body. Both of these must be in perfect working order and under control. These two aspects will be discussed in detail in the next two chapters.

6 Movement and Improvisation

Getting into Character

Our society unfortunately has certain stereotypes about body types. All you need to do is look at the portrayals of body types presented in the media. There is only so much an actor can do about his or her body type, but what can be controlled is how that body moves.

Everyone envies the person who seems to move with grace. When you watch dancers and athletes, their movements seem effortless, but all of this ease comes from years of intense practice. Since actors need the same kind of control, they also must be in shape.

The first step in body control is the actor's awareness of his or her own body movement and how it differs from the character's. Everyone moves in a different way. Can you tell which member of your family is walking down the stairs just by hearing their footsteps? Can you recognize which of your friends is walking to the bus stop just by the way they move? What is the giveaway? What clues in posture and movement determine the individual?

Activity One

Choose someone you know personally. What makes his or her movements unique? What is that person's posture like? Is the person graceful, awkward, athletic? When the person walks, is the tread heavy or light? Is the gait bouncy, gliding, stumbling, jerky, uncertain, plodding? Are there certain gestures that you associate with the person? Are the gestures broad and expansive or close and timid?

As you look at the above exercise, you begin to realize that movement is an important part of a real person's identity; so it is with a character.

Sometimes movement is dictated by an essential point of character; for example, Laura Wingfield's limp in *The Glass Menagerie* or Agnes Gooch's pregnancy in *Mame*.

More often you have to judge how a character moves by the general impression garnered from the play.

Activity Two

Adopt one of the following character types and walk across the stage as that character.

1. A swaggering swordsman
2. A miserly old man
3. A shy, awkward, young girl
4. A pompous, ridiculous older woman

Although there is much more depth to their characters, you may have just begun to develop Cyrano de Bergerac, or Harpagon from Molière's *The Miser*, or Frankie from *A Member of the Wedding*, or Lady Bracknell from *The Importance of Being Ernest*.

Factors of Movement

Aside from costuming, which has a definite effect on how you move on stage, there are several factors you need to consider in a character's movement. These include gender, age, physical condition, personality/attitude, and social norms.

Gender

There is a difference in the way men and women move, or at least in the movements that are considered masculine and feminine. These differences are evident in the way men and women move, stand, and sit.

Age

As one gets older, there is less vitality or spring in the step. Still, you must be especially careful not to stereotype every elderly character as feeble or doddering. No two teenagers move in quite the same way; neither do any two eighty-year-olds.

Physical Condition

Often the most important character consideration at any age is physical condition. Does the character have an infirmity which has been referred to in the script? Does the character's occupation or background indicate a very active or very sedentary lifestyle? Does the information given in the script suggest robust good health or a more delicate constitution?

Personality/Attitude

Emotions affect the way a character moves. Is the character confident or uncertain? Is the character an introvert or an extrovert? Is the character honest or sneaky? Is the character energetic or lazy? Is the character easygoing or contentious? All of these personality traits and attitudes greatly affect movement.

Social Norms

Social norms often impact the way a character moves. A young nobleman in a Molière comedy moves far more stiffly than a young cowboy in *Oklahoma!* A young woman in Victorian England was expected to sit and stand in a more ladylike fashion than would be deemed necessary today. As Anna in *The King and I* must adjust to certain social norms (no one's head is ever to be higher than the king's), so the actor must accurately portray the norms of the society in which the character exists.

Once you have determined the character's general range of movement, you can begin to fine-tune the movement in certain situations.

Activity Three

As a class, put yourself in the following situations.

1. Waiting for a bus on a cold winter morning
2. Waiting in line for frozen yogurt on a hot afternoon
3. Walking barefoot on hot asphalt
4. Walking through three feet of snow
5. Wading into the ocean
6. Stepping on a large gob of chewing gum
7. Walking on ice

There are several items in activities that fall into the context of *mime*. Mime has a long history in the theatre. In mime the actor relies entirely upon his or her body with no dialogue to establish the situation for the audience.

Some of you may have seen street mimes or the most famous mime, Marcel Marceau of France. Mimes are so in tune with how their own bodies relate to the spaces and objects around them that they can honestly make you believe they are dragging an elephant on a rope or that they are trapped behind an invisible wall. You will notice that mimes often perform in whiteface. This goes back to Scaramouche, the mime in the old commedia del l'arte performances.

Perhaps you are more familiar with the form called pantomime. *Pantomime* allows more leeway in that the actors may also rely on words, often silently mouthed. You may use pantomime when you are trying to talk to someone across a room full of people or interpret a phone conversation for someone who is only hearing one side of it.

Because you sometimes use simplified pantomime in everyday situations, it is hard to appreciate how aware of imaginary props and surroundings the actor must be to make pantomime work on stage.

Activity Four

In small groups, perform the following activities in front of the class.

1. Pass an imaginary basketball
2. Pass an imaginary softball

3. Pass an imaginary medicine ball

4. Pass an imaginary Ping-Pong ball

5. Eat imaginary popcorn in a movie theatre

6. Become preschoolers eating cookies and juice after naptime

None of these activities seems particularly difficult at first glance. In fact, you probably have participated in most of them. But what happens in pantomime? You begin to lose concentration on how the objects feel, their size and density. Did the basketball become progressively smaller and the medicine ball much lighter as it moved around the room? Did the preschoolers start out with nice firm cartons or glasses and end up drinking from tiny cylinders held by over-lapping thumbs and forefingers?

In real life, objects don't diminish in size or change weight. They cannot do so in pantomime either. Pantomime requires intense concentration, always keeping in mind what the real objects and the real spaces are like.

Some plays make considerable use of pantomime. One of the most frequently produced is Thornton Wilder's *Our Town*. In this famous play about life in the small town of Grover's Corners, New Hampshire, characters do everything—eat meals, play games, get married—without the benefit of props, a special challenge for the actors.

The more physical control an actor has, the better. Many actors take dance and stage-movement classes to become stronger, more flexible, and more in control of their bodies. Some scenes on stage require special lessons in movement. A fight scene or a fencing scene that takes less than a minute on stage may take days to choreograph because it must be as precise as a dance sequence, and control is essential to keep people from being hurt.

Improvising During Rehearsal

By the time a play is ready to open, everything is set. No one on stage should have to deal with any surprises. However, the rehearsal process is a wonderful time for improvisation.

Improvisation is taking a situation (or scenario) and characters, then inventing the dialogue and activities that would seem to grow naturally from these characters meeting in this situation. This type of improvisation was the backbone of commedia del l'arte and is still the basis for many comedy troupes. It has a real value in helping actors realize how dialogue and movement are natural outgrowths of situation.

Activity Five

Improvise one of the following situations in front of the class.

1. A tired host trying to get the last guest to leave

2. A teen-ager explaining to a parent how the family car got wrecked

3. A child talking to Santa Claus

4. A boy who is allergic to his girlfriend's cat

5. A furniture mover and a client who keeps changing his mind about where things go

6. A teacher accusing a student of plagiarizing a paper
7. Two girls who have a crush on the same boy
8. A parent having a "facts of life" talk with a teen-ager
9. A teen-ager worried about a friend's depression
10. A young couple planning to elope

You may find that the improvisation was difficult to begin and that once it was under way it took many twists and turns. The hardest thing may have been resolving the scenario, bringing it to a close.

Some Off-Broadway plays are based upon improvisation with the audience participating in choosing the course of events and the final outcome. *The Mystery of Edwin Drood* has several different outcomes and each night's final resolution depends upon whom the audience labels as the murderer.

Improvisation is a difficult and specialized art. Most plays are scripted so that the dialogue, plot, and resolution are already established. Still, each night's audience must feel that the action on stage is spontaneous and that they are seeing it happen for the first time. Improvisation helps put the actor in touch with that spontaneity, which the audience must continue to feel while watching the performance—long after rehearsals have set the action on the stage.

7 Voice and Interpretation

Elements of Vocal Interpretation

When someone you have never met before calls you on the phone, what kind of an impact does the voice have? Do you immediately form a mental picture of that person? Similarly, do you have a favorite radio disc jockey that you have never seen in person? Do you always put a face with that voice? What helps you imagine what that person looks like?

Of course the voice can reveal certain characteristics about a person such as age or gender, but we often attribute physical characteristics to a person based upon our own stereotypes of voices. When you finally meet the voice at the other end of the phone or see the radio personality in person, you may be surprised to find that the voice does not match your image of the person.

Activity One

Think about people you know personally or actors whose voices you hear frequently. Remember, you are dealing only with voices.

1. Who has the most soothing voice?
2. Who has the most irritating voice?
3. Who has the happiest voice?
4. Who has the most intimidating voice?
5. Who has the harshest voice?
6. Who has the most authoritative voice?
7. Who has the sexiest voice?

Analyze each of these voices. What gives each voice that special quality? Most of your perceptions are based on pitch, tone, articulation, rate, volume, and dialect. Each of these factors will be discussed in detail.

Vocal Characteristics

Pitch

Pitch refers to how high or low the voice is. The voice, just like any other instrument, has a range of pitch. And, as an instrument or a singer is more versatile with a wider range of pitch, so is the speaking voice.

Pitch in the human voice is determined by the length and tautness of the vocal chords. If you are angry or upset and your vocal chords tense, what happens to your pitch? Conversely, notice how pitch falls when you are tired or very relaxed. How would you pitch a very excitable office worker? A very laid-back cab driver? What is your reaction to a very deep voice? A very shrill voice?

Tone

Tone refers to the quality of the voice, its clarity and emotional content. Before you ever knew the meanings of words, you responded to the tone of the human voice. Think about how people talk to their pets. The words of the scoldings or endearments are indistinguishable to animals who lack language, but the intent of the phrases is very clear to them. Often in an argument you will hear someone say, "Don't you take that tone of voice with me." Tone reveals a great deal about one's emotional state.

Activity Two

Choose one of the following words or phrases. See how many interpretations you can give this common word or phrase simply by changing your tone.

1. No
2. I'm sorry
3. Really
4. Yeah

There are certain natural qualities of a performer's voice that may contribute to tone; the nasal twang of Paula Poundstone or Jaleel White; the huskiness of Rod Stewart or Bryan Adams; the soft breathiness of Marilyn Monroe. But even these qualities change under varying circumstances.

Inflection

Part of tone also includes *inflection,* the accent or stress you place upon certain words to emphasize their importance. Sarcasm, for example, relies heavily upon what words in a statement you choose to accent.

Rate

Rate refers to the speed at which someone speaks. What does extremely fast speech indicate about a character? What about extremely slow speech? What emotions do you associate with changes in the rate of speech?

Most beginning actors have problems with speaking too fast on stage. It may help you to remember that you are portraying a character who is saying these things for the first time, finding the right words as he or she goes along; you do not want to be perceived as the actor who has memorized lines and wants to get them out quickly in order not to forget them.

Articulation

Closely tied to rate is *articulation*. This refers to how clearly and distinctly one speaks. There is perhaps no other factor that so quickly stereotypes a character. What assumptions do you make about the person who has clipped, precise diction and enunciates every syllable? What about the person who mumbles and slurs words together? If you think there is no difference in perceptions, imagine the same newscast read by William F. Buckley and Sylvester Stallone.

Dialect

Finally, there is dialect. *Dialect* refers to the accent speakers may have because they are from a particular country or region.

The odd thing is that no one ever believes he or she has an accent. If everyone you grew up with speaks with a Southern drawl, it's the New Englanders who sound funny. Americans refer to an "English accent" as if the English language originated in the United States. While we may differentiate an upper-class British accent from a cockney accent, many people do not realize there is a distinct dialect in Birmingham, Liverpool, and most other English cities. In George Bernard Shaw's *Pygmalion,* Henry Higgins attempts to win a bet by passing Eliza Doolittle off as a very proper young lady. But first he must get rid of her atrocious cockney accent. Higgins, a professor of phonetics, says that based upon dialect he can place any man within six miles, within two miles in London, and sometimes within two streets.

This is not so true in America today. Since everyone listens to the same newscasts, television shows, and commercials, there is a fairly homogenized version of standard American speech, at least among those who make their living at oral communication. The mobility of modern society has also contributed to this relatively standardized speech.

Still, many plays that are flavored by a distinct regionalism or ethnicity call for dialect. It is important to realize that dialect does give a flavor of regional or ethnic speech—it contributes to the illusion on stage. It generally does not, however, attempt to *exactly* reproduce a regional or foreign accent since this might make it difficult for the audience to understand.

As with most stage elements, the most important aspect of stage dialect is consistency. It is very disconcerting for an audience to be watching a very British Oscar Wilde comedy of manners and realize in the middle of the second act that the actors suddenly sound very American.

Activity Three

Choose a dialect with which you are familiar. It may be the dialect of a neighbor or family member, or it may be the speech pattern of a public figure. You may choose the dialect of another region of the country that you have visited recently. Make a note of the specific qualities and peculiarities of this dialect. Write a brief monologue or dialogue in that dialect, then present it to the class.

8 The Director's Responsibility

Pulling It All Together

The actor is the one who fleshes out the character who first appears on paper; the playwright's fictional person comes alive through the actor's voice and body. That character wears clothes and inhabits a world created by costume and set designers. The artifacts of the character's daily life are provided by the prop crew. But all these things do not happen in isolation. There has to be one person in charge of bringing it all together, one person who artistic vision shapes the whole play. That person is the director.

Some directors, such as the late Joseph Papp, bring unique, fresh interpretations to familiar plays. Papp's famous Shakespeare in the Park series often set the bard's plays in different time periods and places instead of relying on the traditional Elizabethan venue. Any new interpretation may be met with delight or dismay, but the interpretation is the choice of one individual. The director becomes the final authority on everything involved in the production.

Choosing the Play

It is the director who chooses the play after considering every aspect of production, including its suitability for the audience and whether it can be successfully cast and mounted by the available talent.

After the play is chosen, it is the director's responsibility to secure performance rights and arrange for paying any royalties that may be incurred. *Royalty* refers to the payments that go to the playwright and his or her publisher each time the play is produced. Royalty payments are strictly enforced because they are the playwright's source of income after the play's first professional run. The copyright on some older plays may have expired, making them part of the *public domain,* meaning they may be produced at no cost. The director must consider this cost factor carefully, especially when dealing with newer plays and musicals.

Casting the Play

The director sets up and conducts auditions that allow actors to read for (try out for) the production. Sometimes you will notice in movie credits that there is a casting director or casting agency. This is feasible in a movie that has a large cast, a large budget, and a coast-to-coast pool of actors to draw from. However, for most theatre productions, it is the director who makes those decisions.

Once the play is cast and the crews to handle props, lighting, makeup, costuming, set construction, and publicity are established, the rehearsal process can begin.

The Director's Assistants

Two important people now need to be appointed. They are the stage manager and the assistant director. The *stage manager* is the person who controls what goes on backstage. He or she is the one who confirms that the set changes are complete, the actors are in place, and everything is ready for the lights to go up. Usually the stage manager communicates with crew chiefs by means of a headset or other electronic device. During the actual run of the play, the stage manager is responsible for running the show.

The *assistant director* usually sits with the director during rehearsals, taking notes for the director and following along in the prompt script to give cues when actors forget their lines. The assistant director must know the show well enough to run a rehearsal in the director's absence.

Beginning Rehearsals

It is the director who sets the rehearsal schedule and enforces it. It is the director who establishes the style of the show and makes sure that everyone is tuned in to the same idea. Early in rehearsal, the director marks off what location each section of the stage represents and exactly how much of the stage the actors are to use.

Blocking

Having set the basic parameters of the stage, the director begins one of the most important production tasks—blocking. *Blocking* is the direction telling actors where and when to move. You will notice that very often the script will give stage directions: *He crosses down left. She exits. He sits upright.* Some directors choose to adhere very closely to the scripted stage directions. Others have actors cross out all stage directions in the script and begin from scratch. Usually some adjustment of the original stage directions is necessary because your set will rarely be an exact replica of the original. This is particularly true if you are adapting for arena staging a play that was originally blocked for proscenium. Often the changes will be made to accommodate the specific space or actors the director is working with.

As the director blocks the show, actors need to write specific instructions in their scripts. Usually these instructions can be abbreviated so that "cross to up left" becomes "XUL," and so on.

The director usually will tell you to move in a straight line rather than a curved line. When you go somewhere in real life, you live by that old geometry-class axiom that the shortest distance between two points is a straight line. This is no different on stage.

The director usually will tell you to move on your lines, in other words to move as you speak. The reason for this is simple. Movement attracts the eye. When you move on your line, you have the audience's visual and auditory focus. On the other hand, when you move on someone else's line, since visual focus tends to be stronger than auditory focus, you unjustly take the focus away from the actor who is speaking.

The director usually will have conversational groupings with the actors standing in triangular formations. This leaves the actors more open to the audience and diminishes the look of a police lineup on stage.

The director is blocking from and watching from the house, so he or she is the one who sees congested traffic patterns, awkward entrances, and bad positions for the exchange of dialogue. Just as the future audience will, the director is seeing the whole picture at all times. The actors must trust the directions and adjustments from the director and remember that their performance will be best when it contributes to, rather than distracts from, the whole.

A Matter of Interpretation

In the early stages of rehearsal most directors allow, in fact encourage, experimentation and improvisation. Actors need time to try different interpretations, especially when they begin to interact with each other on stage. This applies not only to line interpretation, but also to business. *Business* refers to the small physical things an actor does to help establish his or her character. The director may tell an actor to cross downstage, sit, and flirt with the person who is sitting there. How an actor manifests this flirting is business.

It is the director's job to encourage interpretations that work and cut short those that don't before they become habitual. When a director feels that something isn't working, he or she often may suggest an alternative interpretation. How much freedom a director gives the actors to experiment and improvise depends upon the individual directorial style and the experience of the actors.

Sometimes a director has to "rein in" an actor whose interpretation initially worked but then went too far. In many productions, especially in comedy, an actor will hit on an interpretation or a bit of business that is terrific and genuinely funny. The problem is that sometimes as the audience (or other cast members) react with laughter, the actor may begin to play broader and broader until he or she is mugging, hamming it up, and stealing focus from or upstaging the other actors.

The director isn't visible onstage, but every aspect of the production is stamped by his or her vision. When there is a difference of opinion regarding technical aspects or acting, there is one voice that prevails, and it is always the director's.

Activity One

Choose one of the scenes from Chapter Ten. Cast and block that scene. Have your selected actors walk through and read the scene, adjusting their interpretations as you see fit.

9 From Audition to Performance

The Rehearsal Process from Start to Finish

Any production that is presented to an audience represents many hours of rehearsal. Professional productions, especially repertory theatre or summer stock where several plays are performed in a rotating sequence or in rapid succession, may have fairly brief, intense rehearsal periods because rehearsal and performance are the participants' job. As a student, you probably will be participating in a very different theatre experience.

Preaudition Considerations

Most scholastic and community theatre rehearsal schedules acknowledge that those involved have other commitments, such as classes or jobs. Since rehearsals usually are limited to around three hours a day in the afternoon or evening, there may be many weeks of rehearsal. On average, the full-length school or community production will be in rehearsal for approximately one month.

Before you audition for a role or sign up to work on a technical crew, consider this time commitment carefully. Are you going to be able to add this to your schedule and still keep up with classes, other extracurricular activities, and work obligations? What about your personal life? Are your family and friends supportive of this venture, or is this new drain on the time you have to spend with them going to be a source of friction? Once you make a commitment to the production, many other people are depending on your participation. Being late for rehearsals, missing rehearsals, or dropping out of the production is sure to cause ill will. Make certain you have every intention of fulfilling your obligation.

Auditions

Once you decide to become involved in a production, the first step is the *audition,* sometimes referred to as tryouts. Before auditioning you should read the play at least once. This gives you a basic familiarity with the script and the characters. Very often there will be one character, often a major character, who especially appeals to you, a character that you would love to be able to create on stage. By all means audition for that character, but leave yourself open to the possibility of being cast in another role that the director feels you may be better suited for.

Usually you will be asked to fill out an audition form with information including your height, weight, hair color, and other pertinent details. This will help the director remember you out of all those who auditioned. You probably will be asked to list any past theatre experience you have had and any special talents, such as singing, dancing, or juggling, which could be utilized in the production. Most importantly, you will be asked if you foresee any conflicts with the rehearsal or performance dates. Be honest if you know you have an out-of-town wedding or a graduation to attend. The director needs to know now, not a week into rehearsal. Finally, most directors want to know if you will accept any role as cast, if you will only accept a specific role, or if you are also interested in working on a technical crew.

Most often a director will have you read scenes from the play to be presented, letting you read characters you are particularly interested in. Sometimes, however, a director is only interested in hearing voices and observing actors, planning how their talents on stage can best be utilized.

It is important for a director to see and hear actors on stage together. Do two actors look too much alike? Will the audience be confused by the resemblance? Do two particular voices sound too similar? If two actresses are supposed to play sisters, is there a strong enough physical resemblance for the relationship to be believable?

Activity One

Choose a favorite novel or short story. Imagine that you are casting the movie version. Who would you cast in the major roles? Why?

As the above exercise indicates, often an actor's physical appearance affects casting. You may give a brilliant audition, but if the script calls for a character to be a lumberjack or a fashion model, the physical type is dictated. Furthermore, as was previously mentioned, it may come down to how you look and sound next to the other actors cast.

If a large number of actors have auditioned, the director's decision may be so difficult that he or she may call back a limited number of people to take a look at specific actors reading specific scenes together.

If you do not get the role you wanted, consider taking another role that may be offered or signing up for a technical crew. It can be a great learning experience and a lot of fun.

Rehearsals

After the cast list is posted and the actors have accepted their roles as cast, it is time to begin rehearsals. The first rehearsal is often a readthrough; the cast sits around a table and reads the script aloud. This lets the actors become familiar with who is playing the various roles, lets the director establish ground rules for rehearsals, and lets everyone know the rehearsal schedule for the coming weeks.

Much of the first week will be devoted to *blocking*—giving the actors directions on where, how, and when to move. Although the set will not be complete, if there is to be a couch on stage, the actors should have somewhere to sit. If the set includes a table and chairs, there must be a substitute until the real thing arrives. If there are to be staircases, platforms, or doorways, their future locations must be clearly marked on stage with masking tape.

Usually a play is blocked in sequence; scene two follows scene one, and so on. Blocking a scene takes much longer than the scene will actually run. The actors, with scripts and pencils in hand, write down their blocking and walk through it. This period is when the director finds out if blocking that worked on paper looks awkward on stage. After each scene is blocked, the director will probably go back and run it at least once more.

After the entire play is blocked, the director may choose to rehearse out of sequence so that only the actors involved in specific scenes will need to be at rehearsal on a particular night.

By the end of a week or a week and a half, the actors should know their lines. The first rehearsal without books (scripts) can be rather intimidating, but the director or assistant director will be willing to give you cues for a few days. Sometimes this sink-or-swim method is necessary to separate the actor from the script. If you are one of those hesitant to give up your script, remember that you can never actually begin to work on your character until you surrender your script.

Activity Two

Selecting a play you would want to perform, set up a potential rehearsal schedule. Basically, you will be doing a calendar showing every day from tryouts to performance. Note which rehearsals are for blocking, which scenes are being rehearsed, when lines are due, and when the various technical aspects will be added.

Working Rehearsals

By the time actors are working without scripts, every prop, or at least substitute props, should be there for the actors to work with. Similarly any costume piece that is significantly different from the actor's normal attire should be added; for example, a long rehearsal skirt or dress shoes.

Once the lines are learned and the blocking is established, the real work begins. Are the actors giving the lines the right inflection? Is the play moving at the proper pace? Are the actions and gestures consistent with the lines the characters are saying? Are the characters listening to and interacting with each other? Where are the snags that need to be addressed?

At this point in rehearsal, the director frequently will be stopping to clean up trouble spots before the actors fall into faulty patterns. Sometimes an entire three-hour rehearsal will revolve around one troublesome scene.

About ten days before the play opens, the director probably will begin running the play sequentially so that the cast and crew can get a feel for the order in which things happen. Since there will no doubt still be rough spots to be worked out, the director usually runs one act at a time, devoting Monday's rehearsal to act one, Tuesday's to act two, and so on.

Final Rehearsals

A week before the play opens, complete runthroughs begin. By now all props and costumes should be the actual ones. The set is complete, the lighting is set, music and sound cues have been added. Now there is no stopping the show. If someone forgets a line or a prop, it has to be dealt with on stage, in character.

So, if there is no stopping, how does the director communicate with the actors and crew? Extensive notes are gone over at the end of rehearsal.

In the middle of this last week, there is usually a technical rehearsal. Actors may get a reprieve from costumes (allowing the crew to repair, launder, and finish any minor trim work), but the emphasis is one the technical—lights, sound, props—making sure every stage cue and scene change runs smoothly.

The night before the show opens (sometimes two or even three nights before) is full dress rehearsal. Everything runs exactly as the show will run opening night; all technical and performance aspects are unfolding just as they will when an audience is present.

By the time opening night arrives, everything is ready to go. The director is able to sit in the audience and leave the backstage details to the stage manager. And with the applause at the final curtain comes the reward for all those long hours of rehearsal.

10 Selected Scenes

Scenes for Interpretation and Practice

The following scenes involve a variety of styles of drama. All may be used for practicing vocal interpretation, characterization, and stage movement. A few may also be used for practice in stage dialect.

Each scene is preceded by a brief introduction that helps to set the scene in its proper context.

From *Romeo and Juliet*
by William Shakespeare

Perhaps one of the most famous scenes in all of theatre, this balcony scene sets up the star-crossed love affair between Romeo and Juliet, who have met for the first time earlier that evening at a masked ball. Although their families, the Montagues and the Capulets, are sworn enemies, the young couple realize that their passion will make them ignore family disapproval.

[ACT II • SCENE II]

ROMEO: But, soft! what light through yonder window breaks?
It is the east, and Juliet is the sun!
Arise, fair sun, and kill the envious moon,
Who is already sick and pale with grief
That thou, her maid, art far more fair than she.
Be not her maid, since she is envious;
Her vestal livery is but sick and green,
And none but fools do wear it; cast it off.
It is my lady, O, it is my love!
O, that she knew she were!
She speaks, yet she says nothing; what of that?

Her eye discourses; I will answer it.
I am too bold, 'tis not to me she speaks.
Two of the fairest stars in all the heaven,
Having some business, do entreat her eyes
To twinkle in their spheres till they return.
What if her eyes were there, they in her head?
The brightness of her cheek would shame those stars,
As daylight doth a lamp; her eyes in heaven
Would through the airy region stream so bright
That birds would sing and think it were not night.
See, how she leans her cheek upon her hand!
O, that I were a glove upon that hand,
That I might touch that cheek!

JULIET: Ay me!

ROMEO: She speaks!
O, speak again, bright angel! for thou art
As glorious to this night being o'er my head,
As is a winged messenger of heaven
Unto the white-upturned wondering eyes
Of mortals that fall back to gaze on him
When he bestrides the lazy-pacing clouds
And sails upon the bosom of the air.

JULIET: O Romeo, Romeo! wherefore art thou Romeo?
Deny thy father and refuse thy name;
Or, if thou wilt not, be but sworn my love,
And I'll no longer be a Capulet.

ROMEO: [*Aside.*] Shall I hear more, or shall I speak at this?

JULIET: 'Tis but thy name that is my enemy;
Thou art thyself, though not a Montague.
What's Montague? It is nor hand, nor foot,
Nor arm, nor face, nor any other part
Belonging to a man. O, be some other name!
What's in a name? That which we call a rose
By any other name would smell as sweet;
So Romeo would, were he not Romeo call'd,
Retain that dear perfection which he owes
Without that title. Romeo, doff thy name,
And for thy name which is no part of thee
Take all myself.

ROMEO: I take thee at thy word.
Call me but love, and I'll be new baptized;
Henceforth I never will be Romeo.

JULIET: What man art thou that thus bescreen'd in night
So stumblest on my counsel?

ROMEO: By a name
I know not how to tell thee who I am.
My name, dear saint, is hateful to myself,
Because it is an enemy to thee;
Had I it written, I would tear the word.

JULIET: My ears have yet not drunk a hundred words
Of that tongue's utterance, yet I know the sound.
Art thou not Romeo and a Montague?
ROMEO: Neither, fair maid, if either thee dislike.
JULIET: How camest thou hither, tell me, and wherefore?
The orchard walls are high and hard to climb,
And the place death, considering who thou art,
If any of my kinsmen find thee here.
ROMEO: With love's light wings did I o'erperch these walls;
For stony limits cannot hold love out,
And what love can do that dares love attempt;
Therefore thy kinsmen are no stop to me.
JULIET: If they do see thee, they will murder thee.
ROMEO: Alack, there lies more peril in thine eye
Than twenty of their swords! Look thou but sweet,
And I am proof against their enmity.
JULIET: I would not for the world they saw thee here.
ROMEO: I have night's cloak to hide me from their eyes;
And but thou love me, let them find me here.
My life were better ended by their hate,
Than death prorogued, wanting of thy love.
JULIET: By whose direction found'st thou out this place?
ROMEO: By love, that first did prompt me to inquire;
He lent me counsel and I lent him eyes.
I am no pilot; yet, wert thou as far
As that vast shore wash'd with the farthest sea,
I would adventure for such merchandise.
JULIET: Thou know'st the mask of night is on my face,
Else would a maiden blush bepaint my cheek
For that which thou has heard me speak to-night.
Fain would I dwell on form, fain, fain deny
What I have spoke; but farewell compliment!
Dost thou love me? I know thou wilt say "Ay,"
And I will take thy word; yet, if thou swear'st,
Thou mayst prove false. At lovers' perjuries,
They say, Jove laughs. O gentle Romeo,
If thou dost love, pronounce it faithfully;
Or if thou think'st I am too quickly won,
I'll frown and be perverse and say thee nay,
So thou wilt woo; but else, not for the world.
In truth, fair Montague, I am too fond,
And therefore thou mayst think my 'haviour light;
But trust me, gentleman, I'll prove more true
Than those that have more cunning to be strange.
I should have been more strange, I must confess,
But that thou overheard'st, ere I was ware,
My true love's passion; therefore pardon me,
And not impute this yielding to light love,
Which the dark night hath so discovered.

ROMEO: Lady, by yonder blessed moon I swear
       That tips with silver all these fruit-tree tops—
JULIET: O, swear not by the moon, th' inconstant moon,
       That monthly changes in her circled orb,
       Lest that thy love prove likewise variable.
ROMEO: What shall I swear by?
JULIET: Do not swear at all;
       Or, if thou wilt, swear by thy gracious self,
       Which is the god of my idolatry,
       And I'll believe thee.
ROMEO: If my heart's dear love—
JULIET: Well, do not swear. Although I joy in thee,
       I have no joy of this contract to-night.
       It is too rash, too unadvised, too sudden,
       Too like the lightning, which doth cease to be
       Ere one can say "it lightens." Sweet, good-night!
       This bud of love, by summer's ripening breath,
       May prove a beauteous flower when next we meet.
       Good-night, good-night! as sweet repose and rest
       Come to thy heart as that within my breast!
ROMEO: O, wilt thou leave me so unsatisfied?
JULIET: What satisfaction canst thou have to-night?
ROMEO: The exchange of thy love's faithful vow for mine.
JULIET: I gave thee mine before thou didst request it;
       And yet I would it were to give again.
ROMEO: Wouldst thou withdraw it? For what purpose, love?
JULIET: But to be frank, and give it thee again.
       And yet I wish but for the thing I have.
       My bounty is as boundless as the sea,
       My love as deep; the more I give to thee,
       The more I have, for both are infinite.
                                    [Nurse, calls within.]
       I hear some noise within; dear love, adieu!
       Anon, good nurse! Sweet Montague, be true.
       Stay but a little, I will come again.   [Exit, above.]
       ROMEO: O blessed, blessed night! I am afeard,
       Being in night, all this is but a dream,
       Too flattering-sweet to be substantial.
       [Re-enter Juliet, above.]
JULIET: Three words, dear Romeo, and good-night indeed.
ROMEO: And I'll still stay, to have thee still forget,
       Forgetting any other home but this.
JULIET: 'Tis almost morning; I would have thee gone:—
       And yet no further than a wanton's bird;
       Who lets it hop a little from her hand,
       Like a poor prisoner in his twisted gyves,
       And with a silken thread plucks it back again,
       So loving-jealous of his liberty.
ROMEO: I would I were thy bird.

JULIET: Sweet, so would I;
        Yet I should kill thee with much cherishing.
        Good-night, good-night! Parting is such sweet sorrow
        That I shall say good-night till it be morrow.

From *Hamlet*
by William Shakespeare

There are many famous scenes from Shakespeare's *Hamlet*. In fact, because of its complexity, many actors view Hamlet as the plum role of a career. Shakespeare shows his ability to handle complexity on all levels with his introduction of comic relief about a most grim subject, death.

In this scene, Hamlet and Horatio are conversing with two grave diggers who are hardened to the more human aspects of the work they do. Notice how Hamlet's attitude shifts from his standing by an anonymous grave, to the discovery of the skull of Yorick, his father's beloved court jester, to the final realization that this grave is being dug for his beloved Ophelia who has committed suicide during his absence from Denmark.

[ACT V • SCENE I]

Enter two Clowns [with spades, etc.]

FIRST CLOWN: Is she to be buried in Christian burial
        when she willfully seeks her own salvation?
SECOND CLOWN: I tell thee she is; therefore make her
        grave straight. The crowner hath sat on her, and finds
        it Christian burial.
FIRST CLOWN: How can that be, unless she drown'd her-
        self in her own defense?
SECOND CLOWN: Why, 'tis found so.
FIRST CLOWN: It must be "se offendendo"; it cannot be
        else. For here lies the point: if I drown myself wittingly,
        it argues an act, and an act hath three branches—it is
        to act, to do, and to perform. Argal, she drown'd her-
        self wittingly.
SECOND CLOWN: Nay, but hear you, goodman delver—
FIRST CLOWN: Give me leave. Here lies the water; good.
        Here stands the man; good. If the man go to this wa-
        ter, and drown himself, it is, will he, nill he, he goes,
        mark you that. But if the water come to him and
        drown him, he drowns not himself. Argal, he that is
        not guilty of his own death shortens not his own life.
SECOND CLOWN: But is this law?
FIRST CLOWN: Ay, marry, is 't—crowner's quest law.
SECOND CLOWN: Will you ha' the truth on 't? If this had
        not been a gentlewoman, she should have been bur-
        ied out o' Christian burial.

FIRST CLOWN: Why, there thou say'st. And the more pity that great folk should have count'nance in this world to drown or hang themselves, more than their even-Christen. Come, my spade. There is no ancient gentlemen but gard'ners, ditchers, and grave-makers. They hold up Adam's profession.

SECOND CLOWN: Was he a gentleman?

FIRST CLOWN: 'A was the first that ever bore arms.

SECOND CLOWN: Why, he had none.

FIRST CLOWN: What, art a heathen? How dost thou understand the Scripture? The Scripture says "Adam digg'd." Could he dig without arms? I'll put another question to thee. If thou answerest me not to the purpose, confess thyself—

SECOND CLOWN: Go to.

FIRST CLOWN: What is he that builds stronger than either the mason, the shipwright, or the carpenter?

SECOND CLOWN: The gallows-maker, for that frame outlives a thousand tenants.

FIRST CLOWN: I like thy wit well, in good faith. The gallows does well; but how does it well? It does well to those that do ill. Now thou dost ill to say the gallows is built stronger than the church. Argal, the gallows may do well to thee. To 't again, come.

SECOND CLOWN: "Who builds stronger than a mason, a shipwright, or a carpenter?"

FIRST CLOWN: Ay, tell me that, and unyoke.

SECOND CLOWN: Marry, now I can tell.

FIRST CLOWN: To 't.

SECOND CLOWN: Mass, I cannot tell.

Enter Hamlet and Horatio [*at a distance*].

FIRST CLOWN: Cudgel thy brains no more about it, for your dull ass will not mend his pace with beating; and, when you are ask'd this question next, say "a grave-maker." The houses he makes lasts till doomsday. Go, get thee in, and fetch me a stoup of liquor.

[*Exit Second Clown. First Clown digs.*]

Song.

"In youth, when I did love, did love,
    Methought it was very sweet,
To contract—O—the time for—a—my behove,
    O, methought there—a—was nothing—a—
        meet."

HAMLET: Has this fellow no feeling of his business, that a sings at grave-making?

HORATIO: Custom hath made it in him a property of easiness.

HAMLET: 'Tis e'en so. The hand of little employment
hath the daintier sense.

FIRST CLOWN: *Song.*

"But age, with his stealing steps,
Hath claw'd me in his clutch,
And hath shipped me into the land,
As if I had never been such."

[*Throws up a skull.*]

HAMLET: That skull had a tongue in it, and could sing
once. How the knave jowls it to the ground, as if
'twere Cain's jaw-bone, that did the first murder! This
might be the pate of a politician, which this ass now
o'erreaches, one that would circumvent God, might
if not?

HORATIO: It might, my lord.

HAMLET: Or of a courtier, which could say "Good mor-
row, sweet lord! How dost thou, sweet lord?" This
might be my Lord Such-a-one, that prais'd my Lord
Such-a-one's horse when 'a meant to beg it, might
it not?

HORATIO: Ay, my lord.

HAMLET: Why, e'en so, and now my Lady Worm's,
chapless, and knock'd about the mazzard with a sexton's spade. Here's fine revolution, an we had the trick
to see 't. Did these bones cost no more the breeding,
but to play at loggats with them? Mine ache to think
on 't.

FIRST CLOWN: *Song.*

"A pick-axe, and a spade, a spade,
For and a shrouding sheet;
O, a pit of clay for to be made
For such a guest is meet."

[*Throws up another skull.*]

HAMLET: There's another. Why may not that be the skull
of a lawyer? Where be his quiddities now, his quilli-
ties, his cases, his tenures, and his tricks? Why does
he suffer this mad knave now to knock him about the
sconce with a dirty shovel, and will not tell him of his
action of battery? Hum! This fellow might be in 's time
a great buyer of land, with his statutes, his recogni-
zances, his fines, his double vouchers, his recoveries.
[Is this the fine of his fines, and the recovery of his
recoveries,] to have his fine pate full of fine dirt? Will
his vouchers vouch him no more of his purchases, and
double [ones too], than the length and breadth of a
pair of indentures? The very conveyances of his lands
will scarcely lie in this box, and must th' inheritor
himself have no more, ha?

HORATIO: Not a jot more, my lord.

HAMLET: Is not parchment made of sheep-skins?

HORATIO: Ay, my lord, and of calf-skins too.

HAMLET: They are sheep and calves which seek out assurance in that. I will speak to this fellow.—Whose grave's this, sirrah?

FIRST CLOWN: Mine, sir.
        [*Sings.*] "O, a pit of clay for to be made
           [For such a guest is meet]."

HAMLET: I think it be thine, indeed, for thou liest in 't.

FIRST CLOWN: You lie out on 't, sir, and therefore 'tis not yours. For my part, I do not lie in 't, yet it is mine.

HAMLET: Thou dost lie in 't, to be in 't and say it is thine. 'Tis for the dead, not for the quick; therefore thou liest.

FIRST CLOWN: 'Tis a quick lie, sir; 'twill away again from me to you.

HAMLET: What man dost thou dig it for?

FIRST CLOWN: For no man, sir.

HAMLET: What woman, then?

FIRST CLOWN: For none, neither.

HAMLET: Who is to be buried in 't?

FIRST CLOWN: One that was a woman, sir, but, rest her soul, she's dead.

HAMLET: How absolute the knave is! We must speak by the card, or equivocation will undo us. By the Lord, Horatio, this three years I have taken note of it: the age is grown so pick'd that the toe of the peasant comes so near the heel of the courtier, he galls his kibe. How long hast thou been grave-maker?

FIRST CLOWN: Of all the day i' th' year, I came to 't that day that our last king Hamlet overcame Fortinbras.

HAMLET: How long is that since?

FIRST CLOWN: Cannot you tell that? Every fool can tell that. It was that very day that young Hamlet was born—he that is mad, and sent into England.
    HAMLET: Ay, marry, why was he sent into England?

FIRST CLOWN: Why, because 'a was mad. 'A shall recover his wits there, or, if 'a do not, 'tis no great matter there.

HAMLET: Why?

FIRST CLOWN: 'Twill not be seen in him there. There the men are as mad as he.

HAMLET: How came he mad?

FIRST CLOWN: Very strangely, they say.

HAMLET: How strangely?

FIRST CLOWN: Faith, e'en with losing his wits.

HAMLET: Upon what ground?

FIRST CLOWN: Why, here in Denmark. I have been sexton here, man and boy, thirty years.

HAMLET: How long will a man lie i' th' earth ere he rot?

FIRST CLOWN: Faith, if 'a be not rotten before 'a die—as we have many pocky corses [now-a-days], that will scarce hold the laying in—'a will last you some eight year or nine year. A tanner will last you nine year.

HAMLET: Why he more than another?

FIRST CLOWN: Why, sir, his hide is so tann'd with his trade that 'a will keep out water a great while, and your water is a sore decayer of your whoreson dead body. [*Picks up a skull.*] Here's a skull now hath lain you i' th' earth three and twenty years.

HAMLET: Whose was it?

FIRST CLOWN: A whoreson mad fellow's it was. Whose do you think it was?

HAMLET: Nay, I know not.

FIRST CLOWN: A pestilence on him for a mad rogue! 'A pour'd a flagon of Rhenish on my head once. This same skull, sir, was Yorick's skull, the King's jester.

HAMLET: This?

FIRST CLOWN: E'en that.

HAMLET: [Let me see.] [*Takes the skull.*] Alas, poor Yorick! I knew him, Horatio, a fellow of infinite jest, of most excellent fancy. He hath borne me on his back a thousand times; and now, how abhorr'd in my imagination it is! My gorge rises at it. Here hung those lips that I have kiss'd I know not how oft. Where be your gibes now? Your gambols, your songs, your flashes of merriment that were wont to set the table on a roar? Not one now, to mock your own grinning? Quite chap-fall'n? Now get you to my lady's chamber, and tell her, let her paint an inch thick, to this favor she must come; make her laugh at that. Prithee, Horatio, tell me one thing.

HORATIO: What's that, my lord?

HAMLET: Dost thou think Alexander look'd o' this fashion i' th' earth?

HORATIO: E'en so.

HAMLET: And smelt so? Pah!   [*Puts down the skull.*]

HORATIO: E'en so, my lord.

HAMLET: To what base uses we may return, Horatio! Why may not imagination trace the noble dust of Alexander, till a' find it stopping a bung-hole?

HORATIO: 'Twere to consider too curiously, to consider so.

HAMLET: No, faith, not a jot, but to follow him thither with modesty enough, and likelihood to lead it. [As thus]: Alexander died, Alexander was buried, Alexander returneth to dust; the dust is earth; of earth we

make loam; and why of that loam, whereto he was
converted, might they not stop a beer-barrel?
      Imperious Caesar, dead and turn'd to clay,
      Might stop a hole to keep the wind away.
      O, that that earth which kept the world in awe
      Should patch a wall t' expel the winter's flaw!
But soft, but soft awhile! Here comes the King.

From *Shakespeare: Through the Stages*
by Jean Battlo

Given the reverence that many English teachers accord William Shakespeare, it is easy to forget that he was a part of the popular culture of his day. He wrote for an audience that ranged from royalty to the very common man.

In this opening scene from *Shakespeare: Through the Stages,* Jean Battlo sets up a meeting between the bard and a stuffy, scholarly "expert" on Shakespeare.

(*Shakespeare comes up the aisle, with lute, sings*)

SHAKESPEARE: It was a lover and his lass,
    with a hey and a ho, and a hey nonino,
    That o'er the green cornfield did pass,
    In springtime, the only pretty ringtime.
    When birds do sing, hey ding ading ding,
    Sweet lover's love the spring.
        (*Stops as if being applauded, takes off his
        hat, bows, then continues*)

Oh between the acres of the rye,
With a hey and a ho and a hey nonino,
These pretty country folks would like,
In springtime, the only pretty ringtime.

        (*A stuffy professor comes on stage
        carrying briefcase and stacks of papers
        and goes to lectern. The professor
        looks through pages; Shakespeare looks
        over, but concludes from* As You Like It.*)*

When birds do sing, hey ding ading ding
Sweet lovers love the spring.

PROFESSOR: (*Tries to quiet him*) Ah hem, ah hem, hem!

SHAKESPEARE: (*Continues*) The carol they began that hour,
    With a hey and a ho and a hey nonino,
    How that a life was but a flower.

PROFESSOR: (*Adamant*) Ah hem, I say there, please.

SHAKESPEARE: Oh, I'm very pleased, but it's good of you to ask.

PROFESSOR: Ah hem. (*Glances at audience*) Ah hem, hem!

SHAKESPEARE: (*Jovially*) Ah hem, right back to you my good lady. (*To audience*) I don't understand the import of her "Ah hem," but I'll not fault her for that. There are those who claim not to understand me all that well. So (*Waves at professor*) Ah hem!

PROFESSOR: (*Irritated*) Will you please hold down that ruckus!

SHAKESPEARE: (*To audience*) Now you hear there some of the problems with the English language which I found it so necessary to embellish a bit. I mean, I ask you, how does one "Hold down a ruckus"? Are you sure you would know a ruckus if you saw one? And what does a ruckus do, pray tell? Doth one sit upon it? Perhaps one might ride upon it.

PROFESSOR: Sir, I am attempting to lecture with my considerable profundity on Shakespeare here! This is serious business!

SHAKESPEARE: Serious business? And what did you say was the subject of your profound profundity?

PROFESSOR: Shakespeare!

SHAKESPEARE: What, that humbug serious? That odd fellow with the pantaloons surely can't be taken seriously. I think you've mixed him up royally, say with someone like this Mark Twain person. Let me assure you, old Will is not serious business all the time.

PROFESSOR: What did you say?

SHAKESPEARE: Oh he has his moments. But Will was "no Prince Hamlet, nor was meant to be."

PROFESSOR: Will you sit down and shut up!

SHAKESPEARE: (*Goes on like a heckler; to audience*) Can you sit down and shut up! I think that easier than patting the belly and rubbing the head at the same time. Or is it pat the head—

PROFESSOR: (*Interrupts*) You, sir, are an ignoramus!

SHAKESPEARE: Eh ha, old Will's been called worse.

PROFESSOR: Old Will indeed! I am speaking about the renowned Master William Shakespeare the magnificent!

SHAKESPEARE: (*To audience*) Sounds like a circus act. (*To professor*) My sweet Ophelia, please do forgive my affrontery.

PROFESSOR: I will if you'll sit down.

SHAKESPEARE: I'll sit down if you will. But if I sit down instead of my affrontery, you might forgive my abackery.

PROFESSOR: Will you sit down!

SHAKESPEARE: Yes. (*Smiles at audience*) Will will sit.

PROFESSOR: Will will what?

SHAKESPEARE: (*Enjoys wordplay*) Will will do what Will wills Will to do.

PROFESSOR: (*Losing control*) What what what . . .

SHAKESPEARE: What not, I might add. (*Sits*) Now I sit at your will.

PROFESSOR: I thank you.

SHAKESPEARE: I bid you welcome.

PROFESSOR: Now. (*Straightens up, smoothes hair, etc; to audience*) As you know I am Dr. Emerleen McBedFedSted, the world renowned and most eminent expert on the renowned Master William Shakespeare.

SHAKESPEARE: I didn't know that.

PROFESSOR: (*Glares at him, continues*) I come to speak in his behalf.

SHAKESPEARE: (*Applauds*) Bravo! Bravo! Myself I was never an expert on this Shakespeare fellow.

PROFESSOR: Today I will address myself eruditely, with a certain great rigorous aplomb . . .

SHAKESPEARE: (*To audience*) I dress myself, as you see, in yon tights.

PROFESSOR: —as well, I might add, in an assimilitudinal certainty of the monumental, if not to say perhaps the errodingly, and accurately phrased vicissitude, with a vagary—

SHAKESPEARE: (*Leaps up*) Oh my own dear sweet silly Puck but this character doth make mine own ponderous Polonious seem a mute. (*Shouts as Gertrude says to Polonious*) More matter with less art!

PROFESSOR: (*As Polonious answers*) Sir, I swear I use no art.

SHAKESPEARE: (*To audience*) You're telling me!

PROFESSOR: (*Continues*) I wish in my dissertation to address this illustrious and most ingenious and I think it elegantly credible to say, scholarly—

SHAKESPEARE: Ah, what a piece of work is man. Or woman, for that matter.

PROFESSOR: —who are prepared to understand and perhaps to congregate to discuss certain epistemological conglomerates—

SHAKESPEARE: —How ignoble in reason! —in form and moving, how lumpish and droll!

PROFESSOR: —of esteemed philosophies resulting from an arcane concept that heretofore, and this in a manner of speaking, a priori—

SHAKESPEARE: —in action, how like a waterbug! In apprehension, how like a toad!

PROFESSOR: —and it is consequent of such thought that I find it propitious and, may I say somewhat Byzantine, or perhaps it is more Baroque in content, though a seeming and appropriate attitude toward literature in this proverbial genre—

(*During this speech, as was done in his time, old Will takes tomatoes, eggs, etc., from his pouch and hurls them at her*)

SHAKESPEARE: Egad, woman! What a rogue and senseless ass you are!! (*Throws tomato*) Here, here you awful offal!

PROFESSOR: (*Dodges, backs off*) What on earth are you doing?

SHAKESPEARE: I'm doing what any decent audience in my day did, I'm pelting a paltry performer off the stage. (*Continues throwing objects*) Now get off, you bulbous blasphemous badmouthing buffoon! Go, go, get thee to a nunnery or anywhere, but go!!

PROFESSOR: (*Exiting*) No, no, I won't go. I speak of the immortal Shakespeare here!

SHAKESPEARE: Immortal, smortal! I was immortal but you teachers are killing me! (*Unsheathes sword, thrusts*) Now get, fie on you, fiend! (*Gets paper falling from professor's hands and flings them at her*) Go, go! (*Professor exits; he turns to audience.*) Now, I'll tell you about the world renowned Master William . . . (*Catches himself, laughs*) no, no just about Will. About a boy. A poet from Stratford-upon-Avon. That's me, of course. Will Shakespeare, ho. How did you like that wordplay. "Will will do what Will wills Will to do." Let me assure you that Will usually did what Will willed. (*Winks*) Caused him a little trouble of course. Oh, but my great Coriolanus (*Looks where Professor exited*) what bores we mortals can be. World renowned expert on Shakespeare indeed! Thank heaven we had none of those in my days. School was bad enough but at least I didn't have to memorize me. No, I just led an ordinary life. I lived, loved, yes, I cried some, a poet's life. But my dear drowned dead Ophelia, now they have these gigantic biographies about me talking about things that I wouldn't even have mentioned to my wife! And other tidbits like did I really live and if so did I write my works, well I did!! Lived in fact a good full rich Elizabethan life. I never suffered through a sixth period English class delineating my characters. Thing is at your age (*Comes close to look at young man in audience*) I was thinking pretty much what you are thinking about.

From *The Misanthrope*
by Molière (translated by Richard Wilbur)

Just as Oscar Wilde saw the flaws of his Victorian England, so did Molière see through the pretense of seventeenth-century France, with its elegant language and false friendships. In this scene, Arsinoe, a prudish spinster, and Celimene, a flirt who keeps several admirers on a string, decide to give each other some advice for each other's own good.

[ACT III • SCENE V]

CELIMENE: Shall we sit down!
ARSINOE: That won't be necessary
    Madam, the flame of friendship ought to burn
    Brightest in matters of the most concern,
    And as there's nothing which concerns us more
    Than honor, I have hastened to your door
    To bring you, as your friend, some information
    About the status of your reputation.
    I visited, last night, some virtuous folk,
    And, quite by chance, it was of you they spoke;
    There was, I fear, no tendency to praise
    Your light behavior and your dashing ways.
    The quantity of gentlemen you see
    And your by now notorious coquetry
    Were both so vehemently criticized
    By everyone, that I was much surprised.
    Of course, I needn't tell you where I stood;
    I came to your defense as best I could,
    Assured them you were harmless, and declared

Your soul was absolutely unimpaired.
But there are some things, you must realize,
One can't excuse, however hard one tries,
And I was forced at last into conceding
That your behavior, Madam, is misleading,
That it makes a bad impression, giving rise
To ugly gossip and obscene surmise,
And that if you were more *overtly* good,
You wouldn't be so much misunderstood.
Not that I think you've been unchaste—no! no!
The saints preserve me from a thought so low!
But mere good conscience never did suffice:
One must avoid the outward show of vice.
Madam, you're too intelligent, I'm sure,
To think my motives anything but pure
In offering you this counsel—which I do
Out of a zealous interest in you.

CELIMENE: Madam, I haven't taken you amiss;
I'm very much obliged to you for this;
And I'll at once discharge the obligation
By telling you about *your* reputation.
You've been so friendly as to let me know
What certain people say of me, and so
I mean to follow your benign example
By offering you a somewhat similar sample.
The other day, I went to an affair
And found some most distinguished people there
Discussing piety, both false and true.
The conversation soon came round to you.
Alas! Your prudery and bustling zeal
Appeared to have a very slight appeal.
Your affectation of a grave demeanor,
Your endless talk of virtue and of honor,
The aptitude of your suspicious mind
For finding sin where there is none to find,
Your towering self-esteem, that pitying face
With which you contemplate the human race,
Your sermonizings and your sharp aspersions
On people's pure and innocent diversions—
All these were mentioned, Madam, and, in fact,
Were roundly and concertedly attacked,
"What good," they said, "are all these outward shows,
When everything belies her pious pose?
She prays incessantly; but then, they say,
She beats her maids and cheats them of their pay;
She shows her zeal in every holy place,
But still she's vain enough to paint her face;
She holds that naked statues are immoral,
But with a naked *man* she'd have no quarrel."

Of course, I said to everybody there
That they were being viciously unfair;
But still they were disposed to criticize you,
And all agreed that someone should advise you
To leave the morals of the world alone,
And worry rather more about your own.
They felt that one's self-knowledge should be great
Before one thinks of setting others straight;
That one should learn the art of living well
Before one threatens other men with hell,
And that the Church is best equipped, no doubt,
To guide our souls and root our vices out.
Madam, you're too intelligent, I'm sure,
To think my motives anything but pure
In offering you this counsel—which I do
Out of a zealous interest in you.

ARSINOE: I dared not hope for gratitude, but I
    Did not expect so acid a reply;
    I judge, since you've been so extremely tart,
    That my good counsel pierced you to the heart.

CELIMENE: Far from it, Madam. Indeed, it seems to me
    We ought to trade advice more frequently.
    One's vision of oneself is so defective
    That it would be an excellent corrective.
    If you are willing, Madam, let's arrange
    Shortly to have another frank exchange
    In which we'll tell each other, *entre nous,*
    What you've heard tell of me, and I of you.

ARSINOE: Oh, people never censure you, my dear;
    It's me they criticize. Or so I hear.

CELIMENE: Madam, I think we either blame or praise
    According to our taste and length of days.
    There is a time of life for coquetry,
    And there's a season, too, for prudery.
    When all one's charms are gone, it is, I'm sure,
    Good strategy to be devout and pure:
    It makes one seem a little less forsaken.
    Some day, perhaps, I'll take the road you've taken:
    Time brings all things. But I have time aplenty,
    And see no cause to be a prude at twenty.

ARSINOE: You give your age in such a gloating tone
    That one would think I was an ancient crone;
    We're not so far apart, in sober truth,
    That you can mock me with a boast of youth!
    Madam, you baffle me. I wish I knew
    What moves you to provoke me as you do.

CELIMENE: For my part, Madam, I should like to know
　　　Why you abuse me everywhere you go.
　　　Is it my fault, dear lady, that your hand
　　　Is not, alas, in very great demand?
　　　If men admire me, if they pay me court
　　　And daily make me offers of the sort
　　　You'd dearly love to have them make to you,
　　　How can I help it? What would you have me do?
　　　If what you want is lovers, please feel free
　　　To take as many as you can from me.
ARSINOE: Oh, come. D'you think the world is losing sleep
　　　Over that flock of lovers which you keep,
　　　Or that we find it difficult to guess
　　　What price you pay for their devotedness?
　　　Surely you don't expect us to suppose
　　　Mere merit could attract so many beaux?
　　　It's not your virtue that they're dazzled by;
　　　Nor is it virtuous love for which they sigh.
　　　You're fooling no one, Madam; the world's not blind:
　　　There's many a lady heaven has designed
　　　To call men's noblest, tenderest feelings out,
　　　Who has no lovers dogging her about;
　　　From which it's plain that lovers nowadays
　　　Must be acquired in bold and shameless ways,
　　　And only pay one court for such reward
　　　As modesty and virtue can't afford.
　　　Then don't be quite so puffed up, if you please,
　　　About your tawdry little victories;
　　　Try, if you can, to be a shade less vain,
　　　And treat the world with somewhat less disdain.
　　　If one were envious of your amours,
　　　One soon could have a following like yours;
　　　Lovers are no great trouble to collect
　　　If one prefers them to one's self respect.
CELIMENE: Collect them then, my dear; I'd love to see
　　　You demonstrate that charming theory;
　　　Who knows, you might . . .
ARSINOE: Now, Madam, that will do;
　　　It's time to end this trying interview.
　　　My coach is late in coming to your door,
　　　Or I'd have taken leave of you before.
CELIMENE: Oh, please don't feel that you must rush away;
　　　I'd be delighted, Madam, if you'd stay.
　　　However, lest my conversation bore you,
　　　Let me provide some better company for you;
　　　This gentleman, who comes most apropos,
　　　Will please you more than I could do, I know.

From *The Importance of Being Earnest*
by Oscar Wilde

The comedy of manners takes its shots at a specific society. Oscar Wilde laughs at Victorian social climbing with its emphasis on family background. Lady Bracknell typifies the worst extremes of these pretenses. In this scene she is "interviewing" Jack, a young man who is courting her daughter Gwendolyn. Jack seems to be a perfect match, except for one insurmountable problem in Lady Bracknell's eyes: He cannot prove his family lineage because he was "found" in a traveling bag at a railway station.

[ACT I]

LADY BRACKNELL (*sitting down*): You can take a seat, Mr. Worthing.

> (*Looks in her pocket for note-book and pencil.*)

JACK: Thank you, Lady Bracknell, I prefer standing.

LADY BRACKNELL (*pencil and note-book in hand*): I feel bound to tell you that you are not down on my list of eligible young men, although I have the same list as the dear Duchess of Bolton has. We work together, in fact. However, I am quite ready to enter your name, should your answers be what a really affectionate mother requires. Do you smoke?

JACK: Well, yes, I must admit I smoke.

LADY BRACKNELL: I am glad to hear it. A man should always have an occupation of some kind. There are far too many idle men in London as it is. How old are you?

JACK: Twenty-nine.

LADY BRACKNELL: A very good age to be married at. I have always been of opinion that a man who desires to get married should know either everything or nothing. Which do you know?

JACK (*after some hesitation*): I know nothing, Lady Bracknell.

LADY BRACKNELL: I am pleased to hear it. I do not approve of anything that tampers with natural ignorance. Ignorance is like a delicate exotic fruit; touch it and the bloom is gone. The whole theory of modern education is radically unsound. Fortunately in England, at any rate, education produces no effect whatsoever. If it did, it would prove a serious danger to the upper classes, and probably lead to acts of violence in Grosvenor Square. What is your income?

JACK: Between seven and eight thousand a year.

LADY BRACKNELL (*makes a note in her book*): In land, or in investments?

JACK: In investments, chiefly.

LADY BRACKNELL: That is satisfactory. What between the duties expected of one during one's lifetime, and the duties exacted from one after one's death, land has ceased to be either a profit or a pleasure. It gives one position, and prevents one from keeping it up. That's all that can be said about land.

JACK: I have a country house with some land, of course, attached to it, about fifteen hundred acres, I believe; but I don't depend on that for my real income. In fact, as far as I can make out, the poachers are the only people who make anything out of it.

LADY BRACKNELL: A country house! How many bedrooms? Well, that point can be cleared up afterwards. You have a town house, I hope? A girl with a simple, unspoiled nature, like Gwendolen, could hardly be expected to reside in the country.

JACK: Well, I own a house in Belgrave Square, but it is let by the year to Lady Bloxham. Of course, I can get it back whenever I like, at six months notice.

LADY BRACKNELL: Lady Bloxham? I don't know her.

JACK: Oh, she goes about very little. She is a lady considerably advanced in years.

LADY BRACKNELL: Ah, nowadays that is no guarantee of respectability of character. What number in Belgrave Square?

JACK: 149.

LADY BRACKNELL (*shaking her head*): The unfashionable side. I thought there was something. However, that could easily be altered.

JACK: Do you mean the fashion, or the side?

LADY BRACKNELL (*sternly*): Both, if necessary, I presume. What are your politics?

JACK: Well, I am afraid I really have none. I am a Liberal Unionist.

LADY BRACKNELL: Oh, they count as Tories. They dine with us. Or come in the evening, at any rate. Now to minor matters. Are your parents living?

JACK: I have lost both my parents.

LADY BRACKNELL: To lose one parent, Mr. Worthing, may be regarded as a misfortune; to lose both looks like carelessness. Who was your father? He was evidently a man of some wealth. Was he born in what the Radical papers call the purple of commerce, or did he rise from the ranks of the aristocracy?

JACK: I am afraid I really don't know. The fact is, Lady Bracknell, I said I had lost my parents. It would be nearer the truth to say that my parents seem to have lost me. . . . I don't actually know who I am by birth. I was . . . well, I was found.

LADY BRACKNELL: Found!

JACK: The late Mr. Thomas Cardew, an old gentleman of a very charitable and kindly disposition, found me, and gave me the name of Worthing, because he happened to have a first-class ticket for Worthing in his pocket at the time. Worthing is a place in Sussex. It is a seaside resort.

LADY BRACKNELL: Where did the charitable gentleman who had a first-class ticket for this seaside resort find you?

JACK (*gravely*): In a hand-bag.

LADY BRACKNELL: A hand-bag?

JACK (*very seriously*): Yes, Lady Bracknell. I was in a hand-bag—a somewhat large, black leather hand-bag, with handles to it—an ordinary hand-bag in fact.

LADY BRACKNELL: In what locality did this Mr. James, or Thomas, Cardew come across this ordinary hand-bag?

JACK: In the cloak-room at Victoria Station. it was given to him in mistake for his own.

LADY BRACKNELL: The cloak-room at Victoria Station?

JACK: Yes. The Brighton line.

LADY BRACKNELL: The line is immaterial. Mr. Worthing, I confess I feel somewhat bewildered by what you have just told me. To be born, or at any rate bred, in a hand-bag, whether it had handles or not, seems to me to display a contempt for the ordinary decencies of family life that reminds one of the worst excesses of the French Revolution. And I presume you know what that unfortunate movement led to? As for the particular locality in which the hand-bag was found, a cloak-room at a railway station might serve to conceal a social indiscretion—has probably, indeed, been used for that purpose before now—but it could hardly be regarded as an assured basis for a recognized position in good society.

JACK: May I ask you then what you would advise me to do? I need hardly say I would do anything in the world to ensure Gwendolen's happiness.

LADY BRACKNELL: I would strongly advise you, Mr. Worthing, to try and acquire some relations as soon as possible, and to make a definite effort to produce at any rate one parent, of either sex, before the season is quite over.

JACK: Well, I don't see how I could possibly manage to do that. I can produce the hand-bag at any moment. It is in my dressing-room at home. I really think that should satisfy you, Lady Bracknell.

LADY BRACKNELL: Me, sir! What has it to do with me? You can hardly imagine that I and Lord Bracknell would dream of allowing our only daughter—a girl brought up with the utmost care—to marry into a cloak-room, and form an alliance with a parcel. Good morning, Mr. Worthing!

From "Trifles"
by Susan Glaspell

"Trifles" is set in a small Nebraska town in the early 1900s. Sheriff Peters and the county attorney, along with a neighboring farmer (Hale), are at the Wright farm to search for evidence in the murder of John Wright, who was found strangled in his bed.

Mrs. Wright is being held as the chief suspect, so—in this scene in the farmhouse—Hale's wife and Mrs. Peters have come along to straighten up and take a few personal items to Mrs. Wright at the jail. As the men search for a motive, they laugh about the women's obsession with "trifles": frozen fruit, unbaked bread, a badly stitched quilt section—things the two women find very significant.

MRS. PETERS: Oh, what are you doing, Mrs. Hale?

MRS. HALE (*mildly*): Just putting out a stitch or two that's not sewed very good. (*Threading a needle.*) Bad sewing always made me fidgety.

MRS. PETERS (*with a glance at door, nervously*): I don't think we ought to touch things.

MRS. HALE: I'll just finish up this end. (*Suddenly stopping and leaning forward.*) Mrs. Peters?

MRS. PETERS: Yes, Mrs. Hale?

MRS. HALE: What do you suppose she was so nervous about?

MRS. PETERS: Oh—I don't know. I don't know as she was nervous. I sometimes sew awful queer when I'm just tired. (MRS. HALE *starts to say something, looks at* MRS. PETERS, *then goes on sewing.*) Well, I must get these things wrapped up. They may be through sooner than we think. (*Putting apron and other things together.*) I wonder where I can find a piece of paper, and string. (*Rises.*)

MRS. HALE: In that cupboard, maybe.

MRS. PETERS (*crosses right looking in cupboard*): Why, here's a bird-cage. (*Holds it up.*) Did she have a bird, Mrs. Hale?

MRS. HALE: Why, I don't know whether she did or not—I've not been here for so long. There was a man around last year selling canaries cheap, but I don't know as she took one; maybe she did. She used to sing real pretty herself.

MRS. PETERS (*glancing around*): Seems funny to think of a bird here. But she must have had one, or why would she have a cage? I wonder what happened to it?

MRS. HALE: I s'pose maybe the cat got it.

MRS. PETERS: No, she didn't have a cat. She's got that feeling some people have about cats—being afraid of them. My cat got in her room and she was real upset and asked me to take it out.

MRS. HALE: My sister Bessie was like that. Queer, ain't it?

MRS. PETERS (*examining the cage*): Why, look at this door. It's broke. One hinge is pulled apart. (*Takes a step down to* MRS. HALE*'s right.*)

MRS. HALE (*looking too*): Looks as if someone must have been rough with it.

MRS. PETERS: Why, yes. (*She brings the cage forward and puts it on the table.*)

MRS. HALE (*glancing toward upstage left door*): I wish if they're going to find any evidence they'd be about it. I don't like this place.

MRS. PETERS: But I'm awful glad you came with me, Mrs. Hale. It would be lonesome for me sitting here alone.

MRS. HALE: It would, wouldn't it? (*Dropping her sewing.*) But I tell you what I do wish, Mrs. Peters. I wish I had come over sometimes when *she* was here. I— (*Looking around the room.*)—wish I had.

MRS. PETERS: But of course you were awful busy, Mrs. Hale—your house and your children.

MRS. HALE (*rises and crosses left*): I could've come. I stayed away because it weren't cheerful—and that's why I ought to have come. I—(*Looking out left window.*)— I've never liked this place. Maybe because it's down in a hollow and you don't see the road. I dunno what it is, but it's a lonesome place and always was. I wish I had come over to see Minnie Foster sometimes. I can see now—(*Shakes her head.*)

MRS. PETERS (*left of table and above it*): Well, you mustn't reproach yourself, Mrs. Hale. Somehow we just don't see how it is with other folks until—something turns up.

MRS. HALE: Not having children makes less work—but it makes a quiet house, and Wright out to work all day, and no company when he did come in. (*Turning from window.*) Did you know John Wright, Mrs. Peters?

MRS. PETERS: Not to know him; I've seen him in town. They say he was a good man.

MRS. HALE: Yes—good; he didn't drink, and kept his word as well as most, I guess, and paid his debts. But he was a hard man, Mrs. Peters. Just to pass the time of day with him—(*Shivers.*) Like a raw wind that gets to the bone. (*Pauses, her eye falling on the cage.*) I should think she would 'a' wanted a bird. But what do you suppose went with it?

MRS. PETERS: I don't know, unless it got sick and died.

(*She reaches over and swings the broken door, swings it again, both women watch it.*)

MRS. HALE: You weren't raised round here, were you? (MRS. PETERS *shakes her head.*) You didn't know—her?

MRS. PETERS: Not till they brought her yesterday.

MRS. HALE: She—come to think of it, she was kind of like a bird herself—real sweet and pretty, but kind of timid and—fluttery. How—she—did—change. (*Silence; then as if struck by a happy thought and relieved to get back to everyday things. Crosses right above* MRS. PETERS *to cupboard, replaces small chair used to stand on to its original place downstage right.*) Tell you what, Mrs. Peters, why don't you take the quilt in with you? It might take up her mind.

MRS. PETERS: Why, I think that's a real nice idea, Mrs. Hale. There couldn't possibly be any objection to it, could there? Now, just what would I take? I wonder if her patches are in here—and her things. (*They look in the sewing basket.*)

MRS. HALE (*crosses to right of table*): Here's some red. I expect this has got sewing things in it. (*Brings out a fancy box.*) What a pretty box. Looks like something somebody would give you. Maybe her scissors are in here. (*Opens box. Suddenly puts her hand to her nose.*) Why—(MRS. PETERS *bends nearer, then turns her face away.*) There's something wrapped up in this piece of silk.

MRS. PETERS: Why, this isn't her scissors.

MRS. HALE (*lifting the silk*): Oh, Mrs. Peters—it's— (MRS. PETERS *bends closer.*)

MRS. PETERS: It's the bird.

MRS. HALE: But, Mrs. Peters—look at it! Its neck! Look at its neck! It's all—other side to.

MRS. PETERS: Somebody—wrung—its—neck.

(*Their eyes meet. A look of growing comprehension, of horror. Steps are heard outside.* MRS. HALE *slips box under quilt pieces, and sinks into her chair. Enter* SHERIFF *and* COUNTY ATTORNEY. MRS. PETERS *steps downstage left and stands looking out of window.*)

COUNTY ATTORNEY (*as one turning from serious things to little pleasantries*): Well, ladies, have you decided whether she was going to quilt it or knot it? (*Crosses to center above table.*)

MRS. PETERS: We think she was going to—knot it.

(SHERIFF *crosses to right of stove, lifts stove lid and glances at fire, then stands warming hands at stove.*)

COUNTY ATTORNEY: Well, that's interesting, I'm sure. (*Seeing the bird-cage.*) Has the bird flown?

MRS. HALE (*putting more quilt pieces over the box*): We think the—cat got it.

COUNTY ATTORNEY (*preoccupied*): Is there a cat? (MRS. HALE *glances in a quick covert way at* MRS. PETERS.)

MRS. PETERS (*turning from window takes a step in*): Well, not *now*. They're superstitious, you know. They leave.

COUNTY ATTORNEY (*to* SHERIFF PETERS, *continuing an interrupted conversation*): No sign at all of anyone having come from the outside. Their own rope. Now let's go up again and go over it piece by piece. (*They start upstairs.*) It would have to have been someone who knew just the—

(MRS. PETERS *sits down left of the table. The two women sit there not looking at one another, but as if peering into something and at the same time holding back. When they talk now it is in the manner of feeling their way over strange ground, as if afraid of what they are saying, but as if they cannot help saying it.*)

MRS. HALE (*hesitatively and in hushed voice*): She liked the bird. She was going to bury it in that pretty box.

MRS. PETERS (*in a whisper*): When I was a girl—my kitten—there was a boy took a hatchet, and before my eyes—and before I could get there— (*Covers her face an instant.*) If they hadn't held me back I would have—(*Catches herself, looks upstairs where steps are heard, falters weakly.*)—hurt him.

MRS. HALE (*with a slow look around her*): I wonder how it would seem never to have had any children around. (*Pause.*) No, Wright wouldn't like the bird—a thing that sang. She used to sing. He killed that, too.

MRS. PETERS (*moving uneasily*): We don't know who killed the bird.

MRS. HALE: I knew John Wright.

MRS. PETERS: It was an awful thing was done in this house that night, Mrs. Hale. Killing a man while he slept, slipping a rope around his neck that choked the life out of him.

MRS. HALE: His neck. Choked the life out of him. (*Her hand goes out and rests on the birdcage.*)

MRS. PETERS (*with rising voice*): We don't know who killed him. We don't *know*.

MRS. HALE (*her own feeling not interrupted*): If there'd been years and years of nothing, then a bird to sing to you, it would be awful—still, after the bird was still.

MRS. PETERS (*something within her speaking*): I know what stillness is. When we homesteaded in Dakota, and my first baby died—after he was two years old, and me with no other then—

MRS. HALE (*moving*): How soon do you suppose they'll be through looking for the evidence?

MRS. PETERS: I know what stillness is. (*Pulling herself back.*) The law has got to punish crime, Mrs. Hale.

MRS. HALE (*not as if answering that*): I wish you'd seen Minnie Foster when she wore a white dress with blue ribbons and stood up there in the choir and sang. (*A look around the room*) Oh, I *wish* I'd come over here once in a while! That was a crime! That was a crime! Who's going to punish that?

MRS. PETERS (*looking upstairs*): We mustn't—take on.

MRS. HALE: I might have known she needed help! I know how things can be—for women. I tell you, it's queer, Mrs. Peters. We live close together and we live far apart. We all go through the same things—it's all just a different kind of the same thing. (*Brushes her eyes, noticing the jar of fruit, reaches out for it.*) If I was you I wouldn't tell her her fruit was gone. Tell her it *ain't*. Tell her it's all right. Take this in to prove it to her. She—she may never know whether it was broke or not.

MRS. PETERS (*takes the jar, looks about for something to wrap it in; takes petticoat from the clothes brought from the other room, very nervously begins winding this around the jar. In a false voice*): My, it's a good thing the men couldn't hear us. Wouldn't they just laugh! Getting all stirred up over a little thing like a—dead canary. As if that could have anything to do with—with—wouldn't they *laugh!* (*The men are heard coming downstairs.*)

MRS. HALE (*under her breath*): Maybe they would—maybe they wouldn't.

COUNTY ATTORNEY: No, Peters, it's all perfectly clear except a reason for doing it. But you know juries when it comes to women. If there was some definite thing. (*Crosses slowly to above table.* SHERIFF *crosses downstage right,* MRS. HALE *and* MRS. PETERS *remain seated at either side of table.*) Something to show— something to make a story about—a thing that would connect up with this strange way of doing it— (*The women's eyes meet for an instant. Enter* HALE *from outer door.*)

HALE (*remaining upstage left by door*): Well, I've got the team around. Pretty cold out there.

COUNTY ATTORNEY: I'm going to stay awhile by myself. (*To the* SHERIFF.) You can send Frank out for me, can't you? I want to go over everything. I'm not satisfied we can't do better.

SHERIFF: Do you want to see what Mrs. Peters is going to take in? (*The* LAWYER *picks up the apron, laughs.*)

COUNTY ATTORNEY: Oh, I guess they're not very dangerous things the ladies have picked out. (*Moves a few things about, disturbing the quilt pieces which cover the box. Steps back.*) No, Mrs. Peters doesn't need supervising. For that matter a sheriff's wife is married to the law. Ever think of it that way, Mrs. Peters?

MRS. PETERS: Not—just that way.

SHERIFF (*chuckling*): Married to the law. (*Moves to downstage right door to the other room.*) I just want you to come in here a minute, George. We ought to take a look at these windows.

COUNTY ATTORNEY (*scoffingly*): Oh, windows!

SHERIFF: We'll be right out, Mr. Hale.

(HALE *goes outside. The* SHERIFF *follows the* COUNTY ATTORNEY *into the other room. Then* MRS. HALE *rises, hands tight together, looking intensely at* MRS. PETERS, *whose eyes make a slow turn, finally meeting* MRS. HALE*'s. A moment* MRS. HALE *holds her, then her own eyes point the way to where the box is concealed. Suddenly* MRS. PETERS *throws back quilt pieces and tries to put the box in the bag she is carrying. It is too big. She opens box, starts to take bird out, cannot touch it, goes to pieces, stands there helpless. Sound of a knob turning in the other room.* MRS. HALE *snatches the box and puts it in the pocket of her big coat. Enter* COUNTY ATTORNEY *and* SHERIFF, *who remains downstage right.*)

COUNTY ATTORNEY (*crosses to upstage left door facetiously*): Well, Henry, at least we found out that she was not going to quilt it. She was going to—what is it you call it, ladies.

MRS. HALE (*standing center below table facing front, her hand against her pocket*):
We call it—knot it, Mr. Henderson.

Curtain.

From *This Piece of Land*
by Lou Rivers

This Piece of Land is set in rural South Carolina in 1932, in the depth of the Great Depression. The play revolves around a poor African American family confronting two problems. Rosa is dying and her family is in danger of losing their farm, which has been heavily mortgaged to pay for her unsuccessful medical treatment.

The only alternative Rosa's husband, Perry, sees is to go to Mr. Charlie, a prosperous white man who buys up mortgages with the promise that those who have sold to him can pay monthly and buy back their mortgages. Of course, few manage to meet more than the monthly interest and in the meantime they are sharecroppers.

Rosa, however, sees another option. She has sent her son Leroy for Mr. Morgan, the undertaker, to make plans for her own funeral.

ROSA: Sit down, Mr. Morgan. (*he sits.*) Did you figure out the full amount as I told you to?

MR. MORGAN: Misses Tucker, there's plenty of time for us to figure out these things. Aint no sense in hurryin them on.

ROSA: I told you I wanted all that information figured out by the time I sent for you.

LEROY: (*Rises.*) Mamma—

ROSA: (*Waves* LEROY *quiet.*) How much you gonna charge me for that gray casket?

MR. MORGAN: (*Takes his paper from his pocket*) Now, Misses Tucker, you—

ROSA: I mean the one with the golden stars. And the family cars? I figured it would take at least three to hold all of my relatives and closest of friends.

LEROY: By God, it aint natcherel, Mamma! It aint natcherel for us to go plannin our own burial.

ROSA: I guess it aint—when you don't know it's comin—you might look like you's hurryin it on— (*Silence.*) but when you know, Leroy, I don't see why it haint the natcherelest thing on God's earth to do.

MR. MORGAN: The sickest aint always the nearest to the grave, Misses Tucker.

ROSA: How much, Mr. Morgan?

MR. MORGAN: Well—now—you realize you picked one of the best caskets in the house. That casket by itself at least cost five hundred dollars.

ROSA: That's too much!

MR. MORGAN: But I'm gonna let you have it at three hundred dollars though.

ROSA: And the cars?

MR. MORGAN: Each car—let's see—well, it should cost you—say thirty dollars a car—all together ninety dollars.

ROSA: That's three hundred and ninety dollars. What's for the chimes on the hearst?

MR. MORGAN: Well, now—let me see—the chimes ought to be an additional thirty dollars. But, being it's you, I'll say twenty-five dollars. Now let's see twenty-five dollars for the chimes, plus ninety dollars for the car, plus three hundred dollars—all total four hundred and fifteen dollars.

ROSA: Make it a round four hundred dollars, Mr. Morgan! Oh, my God! Here comes Perry. Now let's all make out like we was just talkin. You all set and keep quiet.

(PERRY *enters. He immediately senses something is wrong.* MR. MORGAN *rises.*)

PERRY: Howdy everybody!

MR. MORGAN: Hydo, Mr. Tucker?

PERRY: Howdy, Mr. Morgan? (*Looks from* LEROY *to* ROSA. What's Mr. Morgan doin out here wid his pad and pencil? (LEROY *turns away.*)

LEROY: Mamma wouldn't let me fetch you!

PERRY: (*Turns to* ROSA, *who walks away. Turns to* MR. MORGAN, *who lowers his head.*) Aint somebody's gonna tell me what the buryin man's doin out here on my place? (*Goes to* ROSA.)

ROSA: Perry, I sent for him to come here!

PERRY: Is you shuttin me out on something, Rosa? Why? What you want to see Mr. Morgan about?

ROSA: Perry, can't a woman who knows she's gonna die, make the arrangements for her own funeral?

PERRY: Who's dyin?

ROSA: *I'm* dyin! Perry, I'm dyin.

PERRY: Who said anything about you dyin? (*Turns to* LEROY.) Boy, did you tell your ma—

LEROY: Not me, Papa! By God, I never mentioned a word!

PERRY: (*To* ROSA.) Who told you such an audacious lie, Rosa? Who in heaven's name—

ROSA: Taint no lie, Perry, and if anybody told me, it was you! (*Reads his eyes.*) The deep down hurt inside you told me. You told me in everything you did, in everything you said to me—

PERRY: Oh, Good God, have mercy. (*Walks away.*)

ROSA: (*Follows him.*) Don't you know when you hurt deep you can't hide it from me—Perry, this is Rosa! You's been tryin to hold the truth back ever since the doctor told you months ago.

PERRY: Doctors have been wrong before, Rosa, you know that.

ROSA: This time, the doctors aint wrong! And I know that. You've did your best. You sent me to the hospital and they couldn't do no good! So before I go Perry, I wants to arrange things the way I want them to be . . . I went down last week and picked out the casket I like. I figured with the family we got, we could get by with the three cars. Other church members, I reckon, will donate their wagons and buggies to accommodate those others who wants to follow me to the buryin ground.

(LEROY *takes his handkerchief and weeps quietly.*)

PERRY: Rosa, don't bust my heart wide open! Don't you bust my heart, woman!

ROSA: Leroy, you stop that! Now don't you do that to Perry. (*Goes to* LEROY.) This is the time, boy, to give him your strength, not your weakness.

LEROY: Mamma, please—

ROSA: Taint no tears, no nothing's gonna change what's gonna happen—so we might as well build ourselves to bear the truth. (*Crosses to* PERRY.) You come, Perry, sit down over here. (*She leads* PERRY *to the step.*)

(LEROY *puts an affectionate arm about his father and sits beside him weeping quietly.*)

ROSA: Now, let's see Mr. Morgan, where was we?

MR. MORGAN: We figured the total to be four hundred and fifteen dollars, Misses Tucker.

ROSA: We said four hundred dollars even, Mr. Morgan.

MR. MORGAN: Yes, that's right, four hundred dollars.

ROSA: That's gonna be the cost of my funeral, not a cent over!

MR. MORGAN: If you say!

ROSA: That's what I say! (*She pulls her apron. For a brief silence she watches* PERRY *and* LEROY.)

MR. MORGAN: No floral pieces?

ROSA: Don't worry about the flowers. The Sisters and Brothers of the church will see to that. (*Takes policies from her apron pocket.*) Now, Mr. Morgan, here is all my life insurance paid up to full. Here's the policy for the Pilgrim's Life, the Metropolitan Life Policy, policy for the Freedom Life—all paid up to full: they should total to two thousand and four hundred dollars.

MR. MORGAN: Yes, um!

ROSA: I'm gonna ask you to make a deal with me. If you don't want to do it, you just say so. I don't want no hemmin and hawin about it, if you can't then I'm gonna send for Mr. Kraft at the Sunshine Undertakers—and I'll make the deal with him!

PERRY: No—

ROSA: My God, Perry don't fight me! (*Above* PERRY.) Is it a deal, Mr. Morgan?

MR. MORGAN: (*Flustered.*) Well, now—Misses Tucker—I don't—

ROSA: (*Sharply.*) I don't want no hemmin and hawin, Mr. Morgan! Is it a deal or aint it?

MR. MORGAN: (*More flustered.*) Well, I never had no deal like this before. I don't even know if it's legal.

PERRY: It aint legal! It's a sin before God!!! (*Points the way.*) You get off my place, Mr. Morgan! (*He starts for* MR. MORGAN. ROSA *and* LEROY *struggle to stop him.*)

ROSA: Perry, it aint no sin!. . .

(*Stops* MR. MORGAN *who has been edging away. She breaks into tears but aborts them.*)

And it's legal all right!

MR. MORGAN: How do you know, Misses Tucker? How can you tell?

ROSA: Because it's my life, Mr. Morgan. That's all it's worth. I'm givin it to you in order to save the land!

MR. MORGAN: Misses Tucker, should a piece of land mean so much to you?

PERRY: Mr. Charlie can have this damn land! I don't want it!!

(*A silence. Overcome by tears, he walks abruptly away from* LEROY *who tries to console him, giving the others his back. The others watch his back, seeing him finally gain control.*)

ROSA: (*Quietly.*) Is it a deal?

MR. MORGAN: (*Finally and quietly.*) It's a deal if that's—what you want.

ROSA: Very well then. You go down tomorrow and settle the business with the bank and bring the final papers and the remainders of nine hundred dollars to me— (*They hesitate.*) Thank you, Mr. Morgan! You's a good man! (*She shakes his hand and starts for the house. Stops to observe* PERRY *and* LEROY.) Leroy, you go home to Sadie and the younguns! Me and Perry wants to be alone . . . for a while.

MR. MORGAN: I'll drop you off, Mr. Tucker!

LEROY: Mamma— (ROSA *moves swiftly and exits into the house.*)

LEROY: (*After a moment.*) Papa, we shoulda known we could *never* keep her from knowing. (*He slowly moves towards the exit.*) (MR. MORGAN *crosses to* PERRY.)

MR. MORGAN: You being the man, Mr. Tucker, tell me what to do.

PERRY: (*Lowers his head.*) I wish I knowed . . . (*Looks into the sky.*) I wish I knowed what to tell you . . .

LEROY: Coming, Mr. Morgan?

PERRY: (*More to himself then to* MR. MORGAN.) I wish I knowed.

MR. MORGAN: Mr. Tucker, God help you. I'll go down to the bank first thing in the morning.

(MR. MORGAN *exits.* LEROY *follows.* PERRY *crosses to sit on the step with his head in his hands. The sun sets more. Soon* ROSA *enters. She's smoking her pipe. She stands there watching* PERRY.)

ROSA: Perry?

PERRY: Yes, Rosa?

ROSA: You vex with me? (PERRY *shakes his head.*) Don't be.

PERRY: I'm losing you, Rosa . . . What good is the land without you?

ROSA: Well, Perry . . . (*Sits next to him.*) for one thing, you won't lose the land to Mr. Charlie! (*Silence.*) I reckon—with all the work we put into this land, we have just about paid for it three or more times over . . . and to lose it for a little of nothin—you love this land—you love it like some men love a second woman— (*Silence as the two look over the land.*) We've got the grandchildren . . . they ought to have some home place they can return to—there's Carmen and Thomas wantin to come home for a visit . . . and Leroy with his younguns—This land will be a remembrance—We always said every man oughta have a little piece of land to call his own.

PERRY: But, Rosa, to take your life insurance money—

ROSA: This land is our pride . . . (*Puts her arm around his shoulder.*) Since I was a little girl, each week we paid on them policies. Before I did, my pa did; and since they air called life insurances they ought to go for helpin life! Don't make no sense that all I'm worth should be put into the ground behind me. (*Silence as she studies* PERRY.)

PERRY: (*Alarmed.*) What's the matter?

ROSA: Perry, do you believe in the hereafter?

PERRY: I do!

ROSA: Do you believe that heaven is as light and coolin as a rain shower on a hot summer day?

PERRY: Yes, Rosa, I believe it.

ROSA: And, do you believe hell is there at the end of eternity in all its bleakness and ugliness for wicked men?

PERRY: What you gittin at, Rosa?

ROSA: Oh, Perry, pray for me! I jest can't git it out of my head and heart—Is God any more fairer to us than the white man?

PERRY: Rosa!

ROSA: Perry, I'm falterin.

PERRY: Now don't talk no more like that!

ROSA: Perry, God mustn't be white—God mustn't be white!

PERRY: God aint got no color at all. God is the spirit of love, Jesus lived and was crucified to teach us to love one another, and he was a white man. (*He holds on to her hands.*)

ROSA: Perry, God mustn't be white. (*Holds tightly to* PERRY. *Presently.*) I'm feelin all right now, Perry . . . Look at the sun . . . The day's almost gone . . . Tomorrow, a new day, a new life . . . another beginning . . . (*After a long silence she rises.*) Come on in, and I'll rub your back for you.

PERRY: I'll come.

ROSA: All right. (*Touches him tenderly.*) Don't fret none. I'm all right now.

From *Carwash*
by Louis Phillips

Carwash is based on a logical premise. Pfeiffer takes his car to an automatic carwash. Then something totally illogical happens—his Mercedes seems to just evaporate in the car wash, and neither he nor Joe and Darlene, the two managers of the establishment, can come up with any reasonable explanation.

PFEIFFER: Get me the manager!

JOE: I am the manager.

PFEIFFER: No, you're not the manager. You're a car thief.

JOE: Keep calm.

PFEIFFER: I am calm.

JOE: You're not calm.

PFEIFFER: You're not the manager!

JOE: I am one of the managers. Everyone on the lot is a manager. It's part of a new psychological theory of increasing profits. Make everybody feel the way the owner feels. We learned it from a book about the Japanese.

PFEIFFER: I don't want to hear about the Japanese right now.

JOE: Why? Are they ruining your business too?

PFEIFFER: I don't have a business. And, at the moment, I don't even have a car!

JOE: You have a car. You came in here with a car. You will leave with one.

PFEIFFER: I want to leave with the one I came in.

JOE: You will.

PFEIFFER: Where is it?

JOE: It has to be in there somewhere.

PFEIFFER: It's not in there. I keep telling you. It's not in there. Look!

(*The owner of the carwash enters. She is* DARLENE SILVERMAN. *In her mid-thirties, she is short, with frizzled hair. She wears a blue jumpsuit.*)

DARLENE: What seems to be the trouble here.

PFEIFFER: I want the manager.

DARLENE: I am the manager.

PFEIFFER: Of course. Everybody's a manager in this business. It's something you learned from the Japanese. . . .

DARLENE: What's that suppose to mean?

JOE: He's upset because he lost his car.

DARLENE: He lost his car?

JOE: He lost his car.

PFEIFFER: I lost my car.

DARLENE: You lost your car?

PFEIFFER: What are we talking about here?

JOE: I thought we were talking about losing your car.

PFEIFFER: That's right. That's exactly what I'm talking about. Losing my car.

DARLENE: If you lost your car, what are you doing at a carwash? It doesn't make any sense to come to a carwash without any car.

PFEIFFER: Are you crazy? What are you talking about? I came here with my car. And now I don't have a car. I put it in there (*Points to the carwash tunnel.*).

DARLENE (*to* JOE): What's he talking about?

JOE: He lost his car.

DARLENE: He lost his car?

PFEIFFER: I lost my car . . . in there.

DARLENE: Is this some kind of a joke? You lost your car in there?

PFEIFFER: I didn't lose the car. You lost the car.

DARLENE (*to* JOE): What's he talking about? It's impossible to lose a car in there.

PFEIFFER: You did something to it.

JOE: I didn't touch the car.

PFEIFFER: Somebody touched the car!

JOE: I don't touch the cars until they come out of the tunnel. Your car didn't come out of the tunnel. Therefore, I didn't touch it.

DARLENE (*to* PFEIFFER): See?

PFEIFFER: See what?

DARLENE: He didn't touch your car. So what are you complaining about?

PFEIFFER: What am I complaining about?

DARLENE: What are you complaining about?

JOE: What's he complaining about?

PFEIFFER: Stop it! I don't want you trying any of your charm school stuff on me.

JOE: What charm school stuff?

PFEIFFER: I don't find any of it charming.

DARLENE: I still don't understand what you're complaining about.

PFEIFFER: I told you.

DARLENE: You didn't tell me.

PFEIFFER: I drove my car into this Charm School and Carwash. . . .

DARLENE: It's not charm school and carwash. It's Charm School Carwash. It's owned by a woman named Charm School.

PFEIFFER: There's actually a woman named Charm School?

DARLENE: Of course there is. You don't think that we would actually name a carwash Charm School unless the owner wanted her name upon it. But maybe you think it's funny to make fun of a person's name.

PFEIFFER: Are you the owner?

DARLENE: No, I'm the manager.

JOE: One of the managers.

DARLENE: My name's Darlene. This is Joe. What's your name?

PFEIFFER: Pfeiffer . . . Salten Pfeiffer.

DARLENE: Salten Pfeiffer and you make fun of someone named Charm School?

PFEIFFER: Don't do this to me!

DARLENE: Do what to you?

PFEIFFER: Put me on the defensive. It's you people who are at fault. Not me. I drove my car in here in good faith. Put it on the conveyor belt, got out, came over here, listened to the water, the brushes, and waited for my car to emerge fully cleansed, brand-new as it were. . . .

JOE: And for less than two dollars too. What kind of a bargain is that?

PFEIFFER: But my car didn't come out. What kind of a bargain is that? The $80,000 car wash.

DARLENE: $80,000? What kind of car are you driving?

PFEIFFER: It was designed for a movie star.

DARLENE: Oh.

PFEIFFER: Oh? What do you mean by "oh"?

DARLENE: I mean you can't expect a movie star's car to act like everybody else's car.

PFEIFFER: I expect it to come out of a carwash.

DARLENE: Maybe it's still in there?

JOE: We looked. It's not in there.

PFEIFFER: What is this? The Bermuda Triangle? I bring my car in here and it goes up in a puff of smoke.

DARLENE: Smoke? Did you actually see a puff of smoke?

PFEIFFER: I didn't see anything. I have been waiting for my car to come out and it didn't come out.

DARLENE: Then why did you say a puff of smoke?

PFEIFFER: It was a figure of speech. A way of talking.

DARLENE: Well, don't say it if you don't mean it.

PFEIFFER: I mean it. I just don't believe it. What do you people do? Is it some kind of illusion? Some magician taught you to pluck people's cars out of thin air?

DARLENE: How do we know it happened?

PFEIFFER: What do you mean?

DARLENE: How do we know you actually came in here with a car?

PFEIFFER: Of course I came in here with a car. What else would I bring to a carwash? My laundry?. . . That's what I did. I brought you my underwear and called it a Mercedes.

DARLENE: No need to talk dirty.

PFEIFFER: I drove in here. I put my Mercedes on the conveyor belt. I got out . . . The car went through and didn't emerge.

DARLENE: You can't prove it. I think you would actually have a difficult time proving you actually brought a car in here.

PFEIFFER: I don't have to prove it!

DARLENE: Of course you do. You don't think the owner is going to pay for a car that doesn't exist.

PFEIFFER: Of course it exists. I have it registered.

DARLENE: I mean exist here.

PFEIFFER: He saw me drive it in. (*To* JOE.) Tell her you saw me drive it in.

JOE: I don't know. It was very busy at the time. A lot of cars were coming through.

PFEIFFER: Not an $80,000 silver Mercedes! What kind of racket are you two running here?

JOE: Be careful what you say.

DARLENE: We're not running any racket. It seems to be that you're the one trying to cheat us.

JOE: How long do you think we could get away with stealing people's cars?

PFEIFFER: You're not stealing my car and getting away with it.

DARLENE: No one is stealing your car.

PFEIFFER: Get me another manager.

JOE: We're the only two managers left.

PFEIFFER: Sorry. Somehow I had gotten the impression that everybody on this lot is a manager. It's a Japanese theory.

JOE: You're not a manager.

PFEIFFER: I'm not even the owner of my automobile anymore. I'm going to the police. This charm school is out of business.

DARLENE: Wait . . . Tell me something.

PFEIFFER: I've been telling you something for the past twenty minutes, but nobody seems to be listening.

DARLENE: Just because we're not strong in communications theory, it doesn't mean you have to yell at us.

PFEIFFER: I want my car back.

JOE: That we understand.

DARLENE: We want your car back too. Believe us. It doesn't help the reputation of a carwash to be losing cars.

PFEIFFER: When it comes to reputation, you people are dead. Of course, you can always change your name to Automobiles Anonymous.

DARLENE: It may not be our fault. It may be the manufacturer's fault.

PFEIFFER: How can it be the manufacturer's fault?

DARLENE: Have you ever had the car washed before?

PFEIFFER: What do you mean?

DARLENE: They're always recalling cars for something.

PFEIFFER: Not Mercedes! And not in the middle of a carwash. The manufacturer didn't come in and pluck it right out of the tunnel.

DARLENE: I mean there might have been a glitch in the paint job. Some kind of chemical so that if water is added to it, it just evaporates.

PFEIFFER: Mercedes don't evaporate. Buicks evaporate! Volkswagens! Maybe even a Greyhound bus or two. But not an $80,000 custom-made Mercedes.

JOE: She's talking about the paint.

PFEIFFER: What? You don't think the car has been in the rain?

JOE: You have an $80,000 Mercedes and you leave it out in the rain. You don't deserve a car like that.

PFEIFFER: Oh, I get it. You take it away from me because you think I don't deserve it? Of all the carwashes in the United States, I have to pick one that's Marxist . . . .

From *Frog Songs*
by Jean Battlo

When one thinks of drama, the assumption may be that all dramatic characters are fictional. However, some dramatists choose to fictionalize real people from history.

Through the strange magic of theatre, these fictionalized people often become more real than any historical account could ever make them. Such is the case with Jean Battlo's *Frog Songs,* which sets up a fictional meeting between two famous American writers from New England, Henry David Thoreau and Emily Dickinson.

Although the two were contemporaries in the nineteenth century, it can be assemed that in reality they never met. Thoreau may be best remembered for his retirement to a cabin in Walden Woods, where he penned the journalistic account published as *Walden.* Miss Emily, the belle of Amherst, became a voluntary recluse in her own home. The play surmises that these two talented eccentrics may have had some interesting commonalities. In this brief scene, the two discuss publication and alternative careers, including Thoreau's brief and unsuccessful stint as a teacher.

THOREAU: I imagine our friends expect to hear writers talk of publication.

EMILY: That shouldn't take either of us very long. I only had eight poems published in my lifetime.

THOREAU: But at least an editor critiqued you.

EMILY: And isn't that everything a poet can ever want? And as I told Higginson, his "surgery was not near so painful as I thought." Besides, I think "Publication is an Auction of the Mind."

THOREAU: I know. I didn't have all that much published myself.

EMILY: Did it bother you?

THOREAU: Not much. Of course, I did have a thousand copies of my book printed at my own expense.

EMILY: If I remember correctly, one three hundred were sold.

THOREAU: True. Ah, but then I was blessed with all those literary leftovers. Think of it, I had a "library of over nine hundred books, seven hundred of which I wrote myself."

EMILY: I suppose that's some accomplishment.

THOREAU: In fact, a highly favored American accomplishment, that accomplishment of accumulation!

EMILY: Seriously, it must have been difficult for you. I had my father's wealth and fine home so could write to heart's content. (*Afterthought*) That is when I wasn't baking bread; Edward Dickinson wanted only my bread on his table.

THOREAU: So he ate breads while world literature waited, hungrily.

EMILY: (*Smiles*) But you, you had to work. Had to find occupation.

THOREAU: Occupation. Now there's a demon for devils to work with. I had to find one to support my habit, writing. And I did many things. Gods and Muses forgive me, I was even a school teacher for a while.

EMILY: Not you.

THOREAU: Oh, the depths of human degradations are not fully known. I knew I had to have GAMEFUL EMPLOYMENT. Boards of Education always seemed to me as "gamey" as life gets; so, I was a teacher. Briefly.

EMILY: I think if anyone is going to be a teacher, that's the way to go about it. Briefly. (*Laughs, shakes her head*) Oh, I can just see you with your wilderness soul behind a stuffy, dusty desk.

THOREAU: I was. I was.

EMILY: You. Mumbling great rules and regulations down through sieves of small resisting minds.

THOREAU: I did. I did. You paint all too clear a picture.

EMILY: I imagine you in more trouble than the children.

THOREAU: (*Answers "New Englandly"*) Ah, yep. Seems I didn't do the will of the Board of Education. Which will is not so unlike that will of Almighty God and this Board wanted me to take a board and beat children. (*Begins to prepare desk, chairs, etc.*)

EMILY: So they brow-beat you.

THOREAU: . . . to have me butt-beat children. Actually, I gave in.

EMILY: You didn't!

THOREAU: Did. (*Stands up majestically*) I tried reasoning with them first . . . (*To audience*) If any of you teach, you know what I mean about reasoning with a Board of Education. So, picture if you will. I go in before the Prime Potency, who holds the handle on the purse that pays me.

EMILY: You can't help but have a certain respect for such people.

THOREAU: At any rate, he stops me before I speak with, "Ah (*Mocks*), Ah hem, there, Mr. Thoreau, Sir. . . ." (*To* EMILY) Guess what was wrong?

EMILY: (*Looks him over*) I dare say, your clothes.

THOREAU: (*Starts putting on a coat, tie*) Precisely. Prime Potent nearly befell himself because he thought he saw a patch on me. (*Looks around at his bottom*)

EMILY: Which I dare say was precisely so.

THOREAU: And "there are those who think life's prospects ruined by a patch."

EMILY: While you prefer a "clear conscience to unpatched pants."

THOREAU: Exactly. "Kings and queens who wear their tailored clothes but once can never know the comfort of clothes that fit."

EMILY: To the point, Henry.

THOREAU: Yes. Well, I told him I'd rather not hit children.

EMILY: To which he replied in clichese, "Spare the rod," etc., ad infinitum.

THOREAU: Precisely, and so said Prime Potent, to which I play Prime Penitent (*Mocks*), "Go forth, Henry David Thoreau; I command thee to BEAT THE CHILDREN!!"

EMILY: (*Biblically*) And went he, Henry, thus forth. . . .

THOREAU: (*Takes seat behind desk.*) I go into the classroom. Take my seat and become as rigid straight and non-flexible as a Thoreauvian can become . . . fixing upon my face a most awful, mean scowl (*Does so*) . . . get about as mean a look as I can, and then I shout out, school-teacherly, "NOW THEN YOU, VILLAINOUS MASTER JIMMY COOPER!!" (*Shouts at empty chair; stops, says to* EMILY) I wonder if you would play the part of little Jimmy Cooper.

EMILY: No. No way, no I couldn't.

THOREAU: Course you can. It'll give the scene some dramatic conflict. A little action. That sort of thing. If you'll just play the part of the misbehaving student.

EMILY: (*Glance at audience*) But Henry. I've never acted.

THOREAU: Come now, Emily. You, in that sweet, self-staged solitude of secret white splendor. Dressed all in curious-character of white-mystery. You never acted?

EMILY: (*Suppressing smile*) Well, I'll try. (*Sits in chair with defiance*) I am little Jimmy Cooper, delinquent.

THOREAU: And I'm Henry David Thoreau, teacher-tyrant! (*Gets into role*) Now, then, Master Cooper, if you will recall yesterday last just as I was so masterfully trying to educate you in various and sundry subjugations of vigorous and various conjugations of said grammarations, did you not in fact daydream and LOOK OUT THE WINDOW?!!

EMILY: I did so do, sir.

THOREAU: Ah, ha, you even confess to so heinous a crime, eh?

EMILY: I do so confess, sir. I never lie.

THOREAU: Ah, ha. Then am I to assume that to this dubious and devious felony, to this most august and awesome error, to this near unheard of and incredible deed, that you did so look out that window for some reason?

EMILY: I felt so, sir; yes, sir, I did, in fact feel there was a reason. A just cause, I might say, sir.

THOREAU: (*Bites words*) You tell me that you feel you had cause to ignore a teacher and with good reason look out a window?

EMILY: I thought so, sir, yes, I did most solemnly so believe. Yes. Sir.

THOREAU: For this unbelievably bad behavior being bandied about in the hallowed cloisters of a classroom, you have reason?

EMILY: (*Shakes her head*) I do most solemnly think so.

THOREAU: Then perhaps you will enlighten me to the enlightenment that led you to look out the window.

EMILY: Of course, sir. My august cause was spring, sir.

THOREAU: Spring.

EMILY: Spring.

THOREAU: Just spring.

EMILY: If there be any such a thing as just spring, then yes, just spring, sir. Yes.

From *The Sound of a Voice*
by David Henry Hwang

Perhaps there is no pain greater than that of loneliness and isolation. The two characters in this play are described as a Japanese man and woman in their fifties, but the emotion of the scene is so universal that it takes on almost a fairy tale quality.

He is the visitor who is constantly practicing swordplay; she is the charming hostess. Before this scene, the audience learns that the woman is rumored to be the witch of the wood who enchants and ensnares her visitors. He practices swordplay because he has originally come there to kill her. But all this changes in the week they are together. As this cutting from the middle of Scene Seven opens, they discuss his leaving.

[SCENE VII]

WOMAN: You want to leave.

MAN: No!

WOMAN: All visitors do. I know. I've met many. They say they'll stay. And they do. For a while. Until they see too much. Or they learn something new. There are boundaries outside of which visitors do not want to see me step. Only who knows what those boundaries are? Not I. They change with every visitor. You have to be careful not to cross them, but you never know where they are. And one day, inevitably, you step outside the lines. The visitor knows. You don't. You didn't know that you'd done anything different. You thought it was just another part of you. The visitor sneaks away. The next day, you learn that you had stepped outside his heart. I'm afraid you've seen too much.

MAN: There are stories.

WOMAN: What?

MAN: People talk.

WOMAN: Where? We're two days from the nearest village.

MAN: Word travels.

WOMAN: What are you talking about?

MAN: There are stories about you. I heard them. They say that your visitors never leave this house.

WOMAN: That's what you heard?

MAN: They say you imprison them.

WOMAN: Then you were a fool to come here.

MAN: Listen.

WOMAN: Me? Listen? You. Look! Where are the prisoners? Have you seen any?

MAN: They told me you were very beautiful.

WOMAN: Then they are blind as well as ignorant.

MAN: You are.

WOMAN: What?

MAN: Beautiful.

WOMAN: Stop that! My skin feels like seaweed.

MAN: I didn't realize it at first. I must confess—I didn't. But over these few days—your face has changed for me. The shape of it. The feel of it. The color. All changed. I look at you now, and I'm no longer sure you are the same woman who had poured tea for me just a week ago. And because of that I remembered—how little I know about a face that changes in the night. (*Pause.*) Have you heard those stories?

WOMAN: I don't listen to old wives' tales.

MAN: But have you heard them?

WOMAN: Yes. I've heard them. From other visitors—young—hot-blooded—or old—who came here because they were told great glory was to be had by killing the witch in the woods.

MAN: I was told that no man could spend time in this house without falling in love.

WOMAN: Oh? So why did you come? Did you wager gold that you could come out untouched? The outside world is so flattering to me. And you—are you like the rest? Passion passing through your heart so powerfully that you can't hold onto it?

MAN: No! I'm afraid!

WOMAN: Of what?

MAN: Sometimes—when I look into the flowers. I think I hear a voice—from inside—a voice beneath the petals. A human voice.

WOMAN: What does it say? "Let me out"?

MAN: No. Listen. It hums. It hums with the peacefulness of one who is completely imprisoned.

WOMAN: I understand that if you listen closely enough, you can hear the ocean.

MAN: No. Wait. Look at it. See the layers? Each petal—hiding the next. Try and see where they end. You can't. Follow them down, further down, around—and as you come down—faster and faster—the breeze picks up. The breeze becomes a wail. And in that rush of air—in the silent midst of it—you can hear a voice.

WOMAN (*grabs flower from Man*): So, you believe I water and prune my lovers? How can you be so foolish? (*She snaps the flower in half, at the stem. She throws it to the ground.*) Do you come only to leave again? To take a chunk of my heart, then leave with your booty on your belt, like a prize? You say that I imprison hearts in these flowers? Well, bits of my heart are trapped with travelers across this land. I can't even keep track. So kill me. If you came here to destroy a witch, kill me now. I can't stand to have it happen again.

MAN: I won't leave you.

WOMAN: I believe you. (*She looks at the flower that she has broken, bends to pick it up. He touches her. They embrace.*)

[SCENE VIII]

Day. Woman wears a simple undergarment, over which she is donning a brightly colored kimono, the same one we saw her wearing upstage of the scrim [a theatre screen]. *Man stands apart.*

WOMAN: I can't cry. I don't have the capacity. Right from birth. I didn't cry. My mother and father were shocked. They thought they'd given birth to a ghost, a demon. Sometimes I've thought myself that. When great sadness has welled up inside me, I've prayed for a means to release the pain from my body. But my prayers went unanswered. The grief remained inside me. It would sit like water, still. (*Pause; she models her kimono.*) Do you like it?

MAN: Yes, it's beautiful.

WOMAN: I wanted to wear something special today.

MAN: It's beautiful. Excuse me. I must practice.

WOMAN: Shall I get you something?

MAN: No.

WOMAN: Some tea, maybe?

MAN: No. (*Man resumes swordplay.*)

WOMAN: Perhaps later today—perhaps we can go out—just around here. We can look for flowers.

MAN: All right.

WOMAN: We don't have to.

MAN: No. Let's.

WOMAN: I just thought if—

MAN: Fine. Where do you want to go?

WOMAN: There are very few recreational activities around here, I know.

MAN: All right. We'll go this afternoon. (*Pause.*)

WOMAN: Can I get you something?

MAN (*turning around*): What?

WOMAN: You might be—

MAN: I'm not hungry or thirsty or cold or hot.

WOMAN: Then what are you?

MAN: Practicing.

(*Man resumes practicing; Woman exits. As soon as she exits, he rests. He sits down. He examines his sword. He runs his finger along the edge of it. He takes the tip, runs it against the soft skin under his chin. He places the sword on the ground with the top pointed directly upwards. He keeps it from falling by placing the tip under his chin. He experiments with different degrees of pressure. Woman reenters. She sees him in this precarious position. She jerks his head upward; the sword falls.*)

WOMAN: Don't do that!

MAN: What?

WOMAN: You can hurt yourself!

MAN: I was practicing!

WOMAN: You were playing!

MAN: I was practicing!

WOMAN: It's dangerous.

MAN: What do you take me for—a child?

WOMAN: Sometimes wise men do childish things.

MAN: I knew what I was doing!

WOMAN: It scares me.

MAN: Don't be ridiculous. (*He reaches for the sword again.*)

WOMAN: Don't! Don't do that!

MAN: Get back! (*He places the sword back in its previous position, suspended between the floor and his chin, upright.*)

WOMAN: But—

MAN: Sssssh!

WOMAN: I wish—

MAN: Listen to me! The slightest shock, you know—the slightest shock—surprise—it might make me jerk or—something—and then . . . so you must be perfectly still and quiet.

WOMAN: But I—

MAN: Sssssh! (*Silence.*) I learned this exercise from a friend—I can't even remember his name—good swordsman—many years ago. He called it his meditation position. He said, like this, he could feel the line between this world and the others because he rested on it. If he saw something in another world that he liked better, all he would have to do is let his head drop, and he'd be there. Simple. No fuss. One day, they found him with the tip of his sword run clean out the back of his neck. He was smiling. I guess he saw something he liked. Or else he'd fallen asleep.

WOMAN: Stop that.

MAN: Stop what?

WOMAN: Tormenting me.

MAN: I'm not.

WOMAN: Take it away!

MAN: You don't have to watch, you know.

WOMAN: Do you want to die that way—an accident?

MAN: I was doing this before you came in.

WOMAN: If you do, all you need to do is tell me.

MAN: What?

WOMAN: I can walk right over. Lean on the back of your head.

MAN: Don't try to threaten—

WOMAN: Or jerk your sword up.

MAN: Or scare me. You can't threaten—

WOMAN: I'm not. But if that's what you want.

MAN: You can't threaten me. You wouldn't do it.

WOMAN: Oh?

MAN: Then I'd be gone. You wouldn't let me leave that easily.

WOMAN: Yes, I would.

MAN: You'd be alone.

WOMAN: No. I'd follow you. Forever. (*Pause.*) Now, let's stop this nonsense.

MAN: No! I can do what I want! Don't come any closer!

WOMAN: Then release your sword.

MAN: Come any closer and I'll drop my head.

WOMAN (Woman slowly approaches Man. She grabs the hilt of the sword. She looks into his eyes. She pulls it out from under his chin.): There will be no more of this. (*She exits with the sword. He starts to follow her, then stops. He touches under his chin. On his finger, he finds a drop of blood.*)

[SCENE IX]

Night. Man is leaving the house. He is just about out, when he hears a shakuhachi [a flute] *playing. He looks around, trying to locate the sound. Woman appears in the doorway to the outside. Shakuhachi slowly fades out.*

WOMAN: It's time for you to go?

MAN: Yes. I'm sorry.

WOMAN: You're just going to sneak out? A thief in the night? A frightened child?

MAN: I care about you.

WOMAN: You express it strangely.

MAN: I leave in shame because it is proper. (*Pause.*) I came seeking glory.

WOMAN: To kill me? You can say it. You'll be surprised at how little I blanche. As if you'd said, "I came for a bowl of rice," or "I came seeking love" or "I came to kill you."

MAN: Weakness. All weakness. Too weak to kill you. Too weak to kill myself. Too weak to do anything but sneak away in shame. (*Woman brings out Man's sword.*)

WOMAN: Were you even planning to leave without this? (*He takes sword.*) Why not stay here?

MAN: I can't live with someone who's defeated me.

WOMAN: I never thought of defeating you. I only wanted to take care of you. To make you happy. Because that made me happy and I was no longer alone.

MAN: You defeated me.

WOMAN: Why do you think that way?

MAN: I came here with a purpose. The world was clear. You changed the shape of your face, the shape of my heart—rearranged everything—created a world where I could do nothing.

WOMAN: I only tried to care for you.

MAN: I guess that was all it took. (*Pause.*)

WOMAN: You still think I'm a witch. Just because old women gossip. You are so cruel. Once you arrived, there were only two possibilities: I would die or you would leave. (*Pause.*) If you believe I'm a witch, then kill me. Rid the province of one more evil.

MAN: I can't—

WOMAN: Why not? If you believe that about me, then it's the right thing to do.

MAN: You know I can't.

WOMAN: Then stay.

MAN: Don't try to force me.

WOMAN: I won't force you to do anything. (*Pause.*) All I wanted was an escape—for both of us. The sound of a human voice—the simplest thing to find, and the hardest to hold onto. This house—my loneliness is etched into the walls. Kill me, but don't leave. Even in death, my spirit would rest here and be comforted by your presence.

MAN: Force me to stay.

WOMAN: I won't. (*Man starts to leave.*) Beware.

MAN: What?

WOMAN: The ground on which you walk is weak. It could give way at any moment. The crevice beneath is dark.

MAN: Are you talking about death? I'm ready to die.

WOMAN: Fear for what is worse than death.

MAN: What?

WOMAN: Falling. Falling through the darkness. Waiting to hit the ground. Picking up speed. Waiting for the ground. Falling faster. Falling alone. Waiting. Falling. Waiting. Falling.

(*Woman wails and runs out through the door to her room. Man stands, confused, not knowing what to do. He starts to follow her, then hesitates, and rushes out the door to the outside. Silence. Slowly, he reenters from the outside. He looks for her in the main room. He goes slowly towards the panel to her room. He throws down his sword. He opens the panel. He goes inside. He comes out. He unrolls his mat. He sits on it, cross-legged. He looks out into space. He notices near him a shakuhachi. He picks it up. He begins to blow into it. He tries to make sounds. He continues trying through the end of the play. The upstage scrim lights up. Upstage, we see the Woman. She is young. She is hanging from a rope suspended from the roof. She has hung herself. Around her are scores of vases with flowers in them whose blossoms have been blown off. Only the stems remain in the vases. Around her swirl the thousands of petals from the flowers. They fill the upstage scrim area like a blizzard of color. Man continues to attempt to play. Lights fade to black.*)

From *Black Elk Speaks*
adapted for the stage by Christopher Sergel
from the book by John G. Neihardt

Black Elk Speaks is the episodic story of the mistreatment of the Native American peoples from the arrival of Columbus through the westward expansion. Perhaps no scene in the play is as poignant as the story of Yellow Woman, a Cheyenne woman who is married to a white man named William Bent.

YELLOW WOMAN (*after turning to the audience*). I'm known as Yellow Woman, and my blood is pure Cheyenne. My husband, however, is white. The blood of our children, of course, is half-his, half-Cheyenne. The name of my husband is Little White Man, but he is also called . . . (*She pronounces it carefully so you will understand.*) . . . William Bent. A man of importance. There are three sons; all with unusual names—Robert, George and Charles. (*She speaks with great pride.*) We live on what is called a ranch.

(BLACK KETTLE, *an old, but active, axe-faced Indian, enters R on the platform. He carries a large American flag of the period which he seems to be planting in the ground.* YELLOW WOMAN *notices his entrance above her.*)

YELLOW WOMAN. Black Kettle is a chief of the Southern Cheyenne. He tries every way to avoid the slightest provocation! We know what happened to the Santees, so he's especially careful to keep the young men busy all the time and out of trouble. If trouble comes anyway, we can depend on two things to protect us. (*She indicates.*) Colonel Greenwood gave this magical flag to Black Kettle and explained that as long as we display it, no soldier will ever fire on us. (BLACK KETTLE, *having planted the flag, hurries down the steps from the platform to* YELLOW WOMAN.) The Cheyenne also depend on my husband—the Little White Man.

BLACK KETTLE. Where can a messenger find him?

YELLOW WOMAN. He could be on the trail from Fort Lyon. Is it trouble?

BLACK KETTLE. Lean Bear brought it on himself. Some soldiers were approaching and he rode out to greet them. (*Concerned about the implications*). The soldiers must be under new orders. They opened fire without warning. They shot Lean Bear out of his horse. (*He starts off R, speaking anxiously.*) Find Little White Man. Tell him we do not know what the shooting was about. I need to talk with him. (*He pauses R, then speaks with utter conviction, half to himself.*) We are not able to fight the whites. If we are to exist, we must have peace. (YELLOW WOMAN *looks after* BLACK KETTLE *as he goes off R.*)

(WILLIAM BENT *enters L on the platform.*)

YELLOW WOMAN. This talk does not appeal to young leaders—strong young leaders.

WILLIAM BENT. Hear me, Yellow Woman. The strong young leaders better untie their horses' tails and stay very quiet. (*He is concerned.*) Where are my sons?

YELLOW WOMAN. Hunting on the Smokey Hill.

WILLIAM BENT. Good. I hope they stay there. (*He is disturbed.*) Colonel Chivington gave orders for his soldiers to kill Cheyennes wherever found. I ruined my horse getting to Chivington to explain that Black Kettle desires only to be friendly. He replied that he was not authorized to make peace and that he is on the warpath! What kind of talk is this?

YELLOW WOMAN (*anxiously*). Our sons must stay out of danger.

WILLIAM BENT. There is no out-of-danger. There's madness in these men!

YELLOW WOMAN. Not all of them. The officer commanding Fort Lyon might help—Tall Chief Wynkoop.

WILLIAM BENT. Major Wynkoop is a decent man. (*Deciding, he hurries down the steps and cross to* YELLOW WOMAN.) I'd better talk with Wynkoop right away. (*He embraces* YELLOW WOMAN.) Stay close to the ranch and avoid all white men.

YELLOW WOMAN (*amused, touching* BENT's *face with affection*). That's not entirely possible.

WILLIAM BENT (*exiting, pleased*). Be careful!

YELLOW WOMAN (*looking after* BENT *with love*). The Little White Man is very unusual. (*To the audience.*) This is why the Cheyennes can depend on him . . . and his family can depend on him.

(BLACK KETTLE *enters R on the platform, going toward the flag.*)

YELLOW WOMAN. There was a daring new idea to get the soldiers to stop the killing.

(MAJOR WYNKOOP *enters DL.*)

YELLOW WOMAN. Tall Chief Wynkoop explained he did not have authority. But he would escort Black Kettle to Denver so he could talk face to face with the big chief—and tell him face to face we want peace.

In the intervening scene, Black Kettle meets with Wynkoop and Colonel Chivington. Although Wynkoop and Lt. Cramer bargain in good faith, Chivington betrays the Indians. He suggests that the braves go up to the hills to hunt buffalo, since the Indian camp at Sand creek is in a safe spot, only 40 miles from Fort Lyon. Yellow Woman resumes the story of that fateful day.

YELLOW WOMAN (*speaking factually*). My oldest son, Robert, was also to be at Sand Creek. All three sons would see what happened at Sand Creek. (*A drummer makes the sound of distant horses' hooves.*) The foolish Cheyennes were so confident they had no sentries. Just before sunrise, there was the sound of hooves. It was a few moments before anyone realized they were shod hooves—soldier horses. (*The sound of the horses' hooves gets louder.*)

(A WOMAN *comes on UR and crosses L.*)

WOMAN (*concerned but not frightened*). Buffalo. Lots of buffalo coming into camp. (*She strains to see better.*) No . . . it's the pony herd. They've been frightened . . . (*With growing concern.*) Men on horses. (*She suddenly realizes.*) Soldiers!

(*There are cries of fear as* INDIANS, *not knowing which way to run, scurry this way and that in the dim light. The drumming of the hooves is now very loud.* BLACK KETTLE *enters and goes to the flag on the raised level. With the cry of "Soldiers!" he steps forward to the edge.*)

BLACK KETTLE. Everyone—hear me! Come this way—up by the flag. Do not be afraid! The soldiers will not hurt you! But you must come here by the flag! You'll be safe up here—hurry! (*From both sides,* INDIANS *begin to collect on the platform, huddling together around the base of the flagstaff.*) Here is your protection! The flag is your protection! Trust me! Do not provoke the soldiers! Do not fight! Do not make war! Stand here and you'll be safe! Listen to me— Black Kettle—and you'll be safe! (*At this, there is a volley of rifle fire.*) Soldiers! (*He points frantically at the flag.*) The flag! We were promised! We were given the flag! No soldiers will ever fire— (*Another volley cuts him off. The light on the platform dims off quickly. He is shocked.*) The promise . . . as long as the flag . . . you will not shoot— (*Another volley. The only light now is on* YELLOW WOMAN. *There are distant cries and shots; their sounds mingling with that of the wind which is blowing hard.*)

YELLOW WOMAN (*her voice now hollow, beyond horror, almost beyond all emotion*). I don't know if there was such a high wind blowing or if the screaming was only in my mind. Seven hundred soldiers attacked. There were only thirty-five braves to face them—the rest were away, as they'd been sent, hunting buffalo. The soldiers had been drinking whiskey during the night ride which might explain why they shot so poorly and why a few Cheyenne escaped . . . including my sons. (*She has to swallow before she can continue.*) We might have been more prepared for what was to happen if we'd known what Colonel Chivington had been saying.

(WILLIAM BENT *enters R and stands.*)

YELLOW WOMAN. He urged the killing and scalping of Indian children as well— because "nits make lice!" Nits make lice! If you don't kill the Indian children, they might grow up!

WILLIAM BENT (*calling to* YELLOW WOMAN). Yellow Woman! Yellow Woman! (*He crosses to* YELLOW WOMAN.) Our sons are safe.

YELLOW WOMAN (*without emotion*). I know that, Little White Man.

WILLIAM BENT. But there's such a strangeness. They don't want to talk.

YELLOW WOMAN. They've talked to me. (*Her voice, as before, is beyond emotion.*) As soon as the firing began, the warriors put the families together trying to protect them, but there were so few young men and soon they'd been killed. The women didn't know what to do. A few of them ran out to let the soldiers see they were women. They exposed themselves and they begged for mercy. (*There are sharp raps on the drum.*) Their bodies were mutilated in such a manner—I can't say the words. (*She takes a breath.*) Some of the others tried to hide in a ravine, but they saw the soldiers coming toward them. They were so terrified they tied a bit of white cloth on a stick—then they sent a six-year-old girl to walk toward the soldiers waving the white flag. (*She turns to* BENT.) Can you measure the terror now? The terror that would make women send out a child—a bewildered child walking toward the soldiers waving her flag? (*She "sees" it. Hushed.*) No . . . No . . . (*A sharp rap on the drum and she screams.*) Iiiieeee!

WILLIAM BENT (*going to* YELLOW WOMAN, *desperately concerned.*) Yellow Woman . . .

YELLOW WOMAN (*verging on insanity, clutching* BENT.) They won't let us live! We can't stay here—we can't go there—they want our farm land—our hunting land. We don't have enough to give them. They will want more—they want us dead! There's nothing left but to fight!

WILLIAM BENT (*grabbing* YELLOW WOMAN*'s wrists*). Listen to me! Wife!

YELLOW WOMAN (*breaking from* BENT, *no longer sane, hushed*). We have to fight . . . (*She points at* BENT) . . . Fight all of them.

WILLIAM BENT. I'm your husband.

YELLOW WOMAN. You're one of them!

WILLIAM BENT. I'm not!

YELLOW WOMAN. You're a white man! I'm starting north with my sons.

WILLIAM BENT. They have my blood, too! My sons, too!

YELLOW WOMAN. We are no part of any white man. We're Cheyenne. We go north to look for warriors! Warriors to save our bodies from desecration! (*She goes off. The heartbroken* WILLIAM BENT *turns and goes. War drums begin.*)

Appendix

Career Opportunities in Theatre

Professional and Nonprofessional Outlets for Your Talents

An old joke asks, "What's a synonym for actor?" The answer? "Unemployed."

As with many creative endeavors, it is difficult to make a living in theatre, at least with any degree of consistency. Everyone hears about the actor making a million dollars a movie or ten thousand dollars an episode for a weekly TV series. No one hears about the actor waiting tables a decade later. If you think that's impossible, flip to your cable channel that carries old movies or "classic" TV shows. How many of those actors have you spotted working recently? Even in the midst of success, many actors fear that they will never work again.

True, there are stage, screen, and television acting roles to be filled. In addition to the movies and soaps we see every day or the Broadway plays we look forward to, there are commercials, repertory theatres, summer stock theatres, voice-overs for animation films, and radio commercials. The list seems endless. The problem is that there are a tremendous number of actors auditioning for every one of those roles.

According to 1991–1992 statistics from Actors Equity (the stage actors union), of the 33,500 paid members, only 14,451 worked at any time during the year. Few of those were full-time jobs. In fact, the average member worked 16.7 weeks for an average annual income of $10,676. Figures are just as modest for other performers' unions. If in spite of all this, you decide to pursue a career as an actor, pursue it with gusto; just be prepared.

The situation in technical theatre is a little better. While designing costumes, sets, or lighting plots may not seem to provide as much fame and glamour, it holds more possibilities for steady employment. Yet even in the technical fields, the competition is heavy.

Does this mean that your involvement in theatre must end when you leave high school? Of course not. There are ways to continue working in theatre for the rest of your life.

If you go to college, note that many college theatre departments do not limit participation in productions to theatre majors. Even though some college directors may tend to cast majors whose work they are familiar with and whom they can trust to carry a show, they are always looking for new faces to fill onstage and backstage roles. There are often student-directed productions that are open to new talent. If you are a theatre major, you may even decide that you would like to be involved in educational theatre and teach and direct in an academic environment.

Aside from college, there are many opportunities to be involved in theatre at the nonprofessional level. Most major metropolitan areas have a number of amateur theatre groups. Most small towns have at least one such group. If your town does not, start one yourself. It is not difficult to find people who have had experiences in theatre or who secretly wish that they could have.

And most importantly, don't be put off by that word *amateur*. Look at its root; it is from the Latin verb *amo* meaning "to love." An amateur is someone who does what he or she does simply for the love of it. Hopefully, even those who make a living in the theatre retain that touch of the amateur—the love of what they do.

Theatre provides a chance for play, self-exploration, entertainment, instruction, enlightenment, and wonderful memories. And what's not to love about that?

Glossary of Key Theatre Terms

absurdism. A movement of modern theater in which the traditional elements of plot are overturned in a deliberate effort to mirror the chaos and unpredictability of the modern world. Productions of this movement, popular in the 1950s and 1960s, are referred to as *theatre of the absurd.*

anachronism. Something out of place by time. Lines in a period drama with contemporary slang or political references are anachronisms. Likewise, properties or costumes from the wrong time period for the setting of a drama are anachronisms.

arena stage. A stage that is surrounded by the audience. An arena stage, sometimes referred to as *theatre-in-the-round,* is often at floor level with the audience in tiers looking down at the action.

articulation. The clarity and distinction of one's speech.

aside. A line said so that the audience hears, but the other actors on stage supposedly do not. An aside may reveal to the audience that a character's real thoughts are far different from those which are openly expressed.

assistant director. The person who makes notes for the director and runs the show in the director's absence.

audition. Trying out for a play. Auditions usually include reading scenes from the play to be performed with others who are auditioning.

blocking. Instructions from the director on where and when actors are to move. Most playwrights give stage directions, but these are often modified or completely redone by the director.

business (stage). The gestures and individual mannerisms added by the actor after the director has done the initial blocking.

catharsis. The cleansing effect of good tragedy. According to Aristotle, the purpose of tragedy was the emotional release the audience experienced after thoroughly identifying with the tragic hero's problems and eventual downfall.

cathurni. High platform shoes worn by ancient Greek actors to give them additional height and visibility.

center stage. The middle of the stage. This is the strongest point of focus for an actor.

comedy. Any play with a happy ending. Comedy also implies a light-hearted story which can provoke laughter.

comedy of manners. A play which makes fun of the manners, mores, and pretensions of a particular society.

commedia del l'arte. A form originating in sixteenth-century Italy in which traveling theatrical troupes improvised plays based upon stock characters and familiar scenarios.

conflict. The problem which the main character must solve, the obstacle to be overcome. A play must have conflict, but it can take several forms: the individual against society; the individual against a specific antagonist; the individual against nature; the individual against inner self.

costumes. The clothing worn on stage by the actors. Whether a contemporary or period play, costuming reveals a great deal about characters and their world on stage.

cultural milieu. The norms, values, and mores of a society that influence the setting beyond just time and place.

dialect. The accent and manner of speaking identified with characters from a nation or region.

downstage. The front area of the stage. On the slanted stages of the ancient Greek theatres, this area was truly downstage.

empathy. The ability to relate to a character's emotions.

fantasy. A play where the plot is outside the realm of possibility, often with nonexistent, other-worldly characters.

farce. Comedy which is dependent on a fast moving, complicated, and improbable plot rather than well-developed characterizations.

flat character. A one-dimensional, stereotyped character. Flat characters are often seen in melodrama and farce where action is more important than characterization.

flats. Wooden frameworks covered with canvas or muslin. Flats are joined together to form the basis for most scenery.

floodlights. Large, unfocused lights which can illuminate a broad area.

follow spotlight. An instrument capable of shining a bright, focused beam on a specific spot. Follow spots differ from other instruments in that they are mobile rather than fixed and can literally "follow" an actor across the stage.

footlights. A strip of lights at floor level at the front of the stage. Footlights are found in most older theatres but are rarely used as a primary source of illumination.

gels. Thin sheets of plastic mounted at the front of a lighting instrument to soften glare and create mood with lighting.

genre. A type of literature. Drama is a separate genre from poetry, short story, and novel. Drama may be further broken down into sub-genres including comedy, tragedy, farce, and melodrama.

high comedy. Comedy which relies more on witty dialogue than does less sophisticated physical comedy.

house lights. The lights over the audience section of the theatre. The dimming and illumination of the house lights signal the audience that the play is about to begin or break for intermission.

improvisation. Developing a scene from a premise without the benefit of a script. Improvisation may be used as rehearsal technique or as the basis for performance, as in the old commedia troupes.

inflection. The accent or stress placed upon certain words to emphasize their importance.

makeup. Cosmetics worn on stage to counteract lighting and suggest character. Greasepaint is makeup from a tube blended onto the skin as a base for further enhancing, aging, or character makeup. Pancake is compressed powder base which is applied with a damp sponge as a base. Makeup may also include hair or prostheses. A prosthesis is a latex or putty appliance for more elaborate makeup. Most commonly these may include noses, bald pates, and scars.

mask. Something that covers the face entirely or partially. Masks in theatre had their origin in ancient Greece where they both displayed character and helped to resonate the voice.

melodrama. A dramatic genre that relies more heavily on action than character development, often combining tragedy and comedy. Melodrama clearly delineates heroes and villains. Thick with sentimentality, this form insures that virtue is rewarded and vice is punished.

method acting. Approach developed by Konstantin Stanislavsky, where actors evoke memories and feeling from their own experiences in order to identify the motivation for a character's action and play it accordingly.

mime. Performance of a scene without dialogue. Mime has its basis in the commedia del l'arte. Some performers, usually in white face, specialize exclusively in mime.

monologue. A long speech by one character. A monologue is addressed to another character or characters on stage, or to the audience itself.

morality plays. A type of medieval drama in which the characters are personified virtues and vices and the plot is allegorical, symbolic of spiritual lessons. The most famous of these is *Everyman.*

motivation. The reason behind a character's actions.

naturalism. In theatre, an ultra-realistic form which attempts to portray "life" rather than a dramatic reproduction. Naturalism often views the world as an environment holding the fate of humanity but unconcerned with its well-being.

pantomime. A less traditional style of mime which may even include mouthed dialogue. Many plays incorporate some elements of pantomime, such as Thornton Wilder's *Our Town,* where the characters cook, eat meals, and drink sodas—all without the benefit of props.

pitch. How high or low the voice is.

presentational. Style of theatre production in which the players are clearly aware of the presence of the audience and act accordingly, often directly addressing the crowd.

props. Short for *properties.* Set props are the items set on stage before the play or during the scene changes. Hand props are pre-set on the property table and carried on stage by the actors. Props are as important as costumes and scenery in setting the feel of the play; often they are crucial to the plot itself.

property manager. The head of the prop crew. He or she is responsible for acquiring all props and seeing that they are pre-set or in the actor's possession when he or she goes on stage.

proscenium stage. A stage enclosed by a "picture frame" arch that allows the audience to sit in front and look straight on at the action.

public domain. Plays in which the author's copyright has expired. *Usually* after seventy-five years after publication, plays become part of the public domain, meaning they may be performed without the author's permission or royalty payments.

rate. The speed at which one speaks.

realism. A style of drama that attempts to accurately portray life with careful attention to detail. Realism is often associated with the "fourth wall" concept, whereby the stage is viewed as a real location or room where the audience is able to view the action through an invisible "fourth wall."

representational. Style of production in which the action of the play exists in a world devoid of the audience. Actors never acknowledge the world beyond the "fourth wall," which separates them from the audience.

round character. A complex, multi-dimensional character who is capable of changing and developing throughout the play.

royalty. Payment made to the playwright, publisher, or agent for permission to perform a play, depending on who holds the copyright.

satire. Comedy which makes fun of individuals, institutions, or irritations of everyday life in an effort to change them, or to change society's attitude toward them.

set pieces. Furniture and parts of the set other than flats. The stage crew may add and remove set pieces during scene changes.

stage left/stage right. The left and right sides of the stage from the actor's perspective. Note that stage right and left are the opposite of the audience's right and left. (Often abbreviated as L and R in stage directions in a play script.)

stage manager. The person responsible for all technical, backstage elements of the show.

stereotyping. In theatre and drama, the assumption that a character will behave in a certain way based upon one factor of his personality. One example: all old people are feeble and doddering.

stock character. Characters that have recurred so frequently throughout theatre history that they are immediately familiar to the audience. Many of these characters (the swaggering soldier, the pompous scholar, the sly servant) can be traced from the ancient Roman comedies through commedia del l'arte to the modern situation comedies.

soliloquy. A speech by a character alone on stage. The soliloquy is a dramatic convention that allows the audience to hear the character's true, unrestrained thoughts. One of the most famous soliloquies is that of Shakespeare's *Hamlet* ("To be or not to be . . .").

technical method of acting. "External" style of acting, based upon the old oratorical styles where actors adopt certain postures and gestures typical of an emotion to be played.

thrust stage. A stage which is surrounded on three sides by the audience.

tone. The quality of the voice, its clarity and emotional content.

tragedy. A serious play which concludes with the downfall or destruction of its central protagonist or tragic hero.

tragedian. A writer of tragedies. The term may also be used to apply to an actor who specializes in tragic roles.

tragic flaw. The aspect of a tragic hero's character which leads to his or her downfall (i.e., Macbeth's ambition, King Lear's vanity).

tragic hero. In the classical theatre tradition, a man of great stature who falls because of a "tragic flaw" in his own personality. Modern dramatists are more concerned with the problems of the common man and woman than those of males portrayed in classical tragedy.

tragoedia. The Greek term meaning "goat song." The initial tragoedia in the religious rites to the god Dionysus (Greek god of wine and debauchery) served as the foundation for tragedy.

trilogy. A cycle of three plays. Although each of the three plays is complete in itself, all revolve around the same theme or, more traditionally, follow the action of a family or specific set of characters.

typecasting. Casting an actor because he or she is similar to the character. Most actors love to prove their range by being cast against type.

upstage. The back area of the stage. On the slanted stages of the ancient Greek theatres, this area was truly upstage.

Bibliography and Resource List

Books on Directing

Beck, Roy A. et al. *Play Production Today!*, 4th ed. Lincolnwood, Ill.: National Textbook Co., 1989.

Canfield, Curtis. *The Craft of Play Directing*. New York: Holt, Rinehart & Winston, 1963.

Dean, Alexander, and Carra, Lawrence. *Fundamentals of Play Directing*, 4th ed. New York: Holt, Rinehart & Winston, 1980.

Gorchakov, Nikolai M. *Stanislavsky Directs*. Tr. by Miriam Goldina. New York: Funk & Wagnalls, 1954.

Hodge, Francis. *Play Directing*. 3rd ed. Englewood Cliffs: Prentice-Hall, Inc., 1988.

Stanislavski, Constantin. *An Actor Prepares*. Tr. by Elizabeth Reynolds Hapgood. New York: Theatre Arts Books, 1936.

_____. *Building a Character*. Tr. by Elizabeth Reynolds Hapgood. New York: Theatre Arts Books, 1949.

Staub, August W. *Creating Theatre*. New York: Harper & Row, 1973.

Welker, David. *Theatrical Direction*. Boston: Allyn & Bacon, Inc., 1971.

Wills, J. Robert (ed.). *The Director in a Changing Theatre*. Palo Alto, Calif.: Mayfield Publishing Co., 1976.

Books on Acting

Benedetti, Robert L. *The Actor at Work*. 3rd ed. Englewood Cliffs: Prentice-Hall, 1981.

Cassady, Marsh. *The Book of Scenes for Aspiring Young Actors*. Lincolnwood, Ill.: National Textbook Co., 1994.

Cohen, Robert. *Acting One*. Palo Alto, Calif.: Mayfield Publishing Co., 1984.

Delgado, Ramon. *Acting with Both Sides of Your Brain*. New York: Holt, Rinehart and Winston, 1986.

Felnagle, Richard H. *Beginning Acting*. Englewood Cliffs: Prentice-Hall, 1987.

Harrop, John, and Epstein, Sabin R. *Acting with Style*. Englewood Cliffs: Prentice-Hall, 1982.

Hobbs, Robert L. *Teach Yourself Transatlantic: Theatre Speech for Actors*. Palo Alto, Calif.: Mayfield Publishing Co., 1986.

Kuritz, Paul. *Playing: An Introduction to Acting*. Englewood Cliffs: Prentice-Hall, 1982.

Lessac, Arthur. *Body Wisdom: The Use and Training of the Human Body*. New York: Drama Book Specialists, 1981.

Lewis, Robert. *Advice to the Players*. New York: Harper & Row, 1980.

McGaw, Charles, and Clark, Larry D. *Acting Is Believing*. 6th ed. New York: Harcourt Brace College Publishers, 1992.

Morris, Eric, and Hotchkis, Joan. *No Acting Please.* Los Angeles: Whitehouse/Spelling Publications, 1979.

Shurtleff, Michael. *Auditions.* New York: Walker and Co., 1978.

Snyder, Joan, and Drumsta, Michael. *The Dynamics of Acting.* 3rd ed. Lincolnwood, Ill.: National Textbook Co., 1989.

Stanislavski, Constantin. *Creating a Role.* Tr. by Elizabeth Reynolds Hapgood. New York: Theatre Arts Books, 1961.

Books on Stagecraft and Lighting

Beck, Roy A. *Stagecraft.* 3rd ed. Lincolnwood, Ill.: National Textbook Co., 1990.

Bellman, Williard. *Scene Design, Stage Lighting, Sound, Costume and Makeup: A Scenographic Approach.* New York: Harper & Row, 1983.

Burris-Meyer, Harold, et al. *Sound in the Theatre.* New York: Theatre Arts Books, 1979.

Govier, Jacquie. *Create Your Own Stage Props.* Englewood, N.J.: Prentice-Hall Press, 1986.

Gruver, Bert. *The Stagemanager's Handbook.* Edited by Frank Hamilton. New York: Drama Book Specialists, 1972.

McCandless, Stanley R. *A Method of Lighting the Stage.* 4th ed. New York: Theatre Art Books, Inc., 1958.

Parker, W. Oren. *Sceno-Graphic Techniques.* 3rd ed. Carbondale, Ill.: Southern Illinois University Press, 1987.

_____. *Stage Lighting Practice and Design.* New York: Holt, Rinehart & Winston, 1987.

Parker, W. Oren, and Smith, Harvey K. *Scene Design and Stage Lighting.* 5th ed. New York: Holt Rinehart & Winston, 1985.

Pecktal, Lynn. *Designing and Painting for the Theatre.* New York: Holt Rinehart & Winston, 1975.

Pilbrow, Richard. *Stage Lighting.* New York: Applause Theatre Books, 1986.

Stern, Lawrence. *Stage Management: Guidebook of Practical Techniques.* 3rd ed. Boston: Allyn & Bacon, 1986.

Streader, Timothy, and Williams, John. *Create Your Own Stage Lighting.* Englewood, N.J.: Prentice-Hall Press, 1986.

Thomas, Terry. *Create Your Own Stage Sets.* Englewood, N.J.: Prentice Hall Press, 1984.

Books on Costumes and Makeup

Barton, Lucy. *Historic Costume for the Stage.* Rev. ed. Boston: Baker, 1961.

Corson, Richard. *Stage Makeup.* 5th ed. Englewood Cliffs, N.J.: Prentice-Hall, 1975.

Covey, Liz. *The Costumer's Handbook.* Englewood Cliffs, N.J.: Prentice-Hall, 1980.

Green, Michael. *Theatrical Costumes and the Amateur Stage.* Boston: Plays, Inc., 1968.

Jackson, Sheila. *Costumes for the Stage: A Complete Handbook for Every Kind of Play.* New York: Dutton, 1978.

Prisk, Berneice. *Stage Costume Handbook.* New York: Harper & Row, 1966.

Russell, Douglas A. *Stage Costume Design.* New York: Appleton-Century-Crofts, 1973.

Smith, C. Ray. *The Theatre Crafts Book of Costumes.* Emmaus, Pa.: Rodale Press, 1973.

Westmore, Michael G. *The Art of Theatrical Makeup for Stage and Screen.* New York: McGraw-Hill, 1972.

Full-Length Plays Available for School Productions

Each play is accompanied by a brief description and performance information. See the following key for abbreviations.

> Key to Abbreviations
>
> *M*—Number of men's roles in the play. (ex., 5M—five male roles)
>
> *W*—Number of women's roles in the play. (ex., 4W—four female roles)
>
> *int.*—interior set
>
> *ext.*—exterior set
>
> *contemp.*—contemporary costumes
>
> The above abbreviations are followed by the name of the publisher who holds the production rights. Addresses of the publishers follow the list. The following abbreviations are used:
>
> French—Samuel French, Inc.
>
> DPS—Dramatists Play Service
>
> Dramatic Pub.—The Dramatic Publishing Company
>
> Baker—Baker Plays

The Admirable Crichton, by J.M. Barrie (comedy); 13M, 12W; 1 int.; 1 ext.; turn-of-the-century upper class; French. Crichton, the butler, insists that class distinctions should be maintained and that only a return to primitive society would show who should be master and servant. They are shipwrecked on a Pacific Island and only Crichton's ability saves them. Once rescued, they return to England and their former positions. Crichton sees that the reputation of the family is preserved and then resigns.

Ah, Wilderness! by Eugene O'Neill (comedy); 9M, 6W; 3 int.; 1 ext.; 1900; French. The tender story of a rebellious young anarchist who achieves manhood the hard way, via a saloon. May need deletions.

All My Sons, by Arthur Miller (drama); 6M, 4W; 1 ext.; contemp.; DPS. An intense story of guilt, bitterness, and deception as the lives of two families become entangled following the shipment of defective airplane parts during the war.

All the King's Men, by Robert Penn Warren (drama); 14M, 4W; 1 ext.; 1930s; DPS. Based upon the political career of Gov. Huey Long (La.). The sometimes corrupt but admirable rise from small town idealist to governor. A fine study of character, both of Willie Stark (Long) and a newsman who works for him.

Anastasia, by Guy Bolton (drama); 8M, 5W; 1 int.; several years after the Russian revolution; French. Roguish adventurers hope to gain control of the impounded czarist fortunes by presenting an imposter as the Grand Duchess Anastasia, but ensuing events suggest that the girl they have found may not be an imposter.

Androcles and the Lion, by George Bernard Shaw (comedy); 19M, 2W; multiple setting; Baker. Somewhat satirical treatment of the thorn-in-a-lion's-paw story.

Angel Street, by Patrick Hamilton (melodrama); 2M, 3W; 1 int.; 1880; French. Tension mounts as a wanted murderer nearly succeeds in convincing his wife that she is insane.

Anne of the Thousand Days, by Maxwell Anderson (romantic drama); 11M, 5W; unit set; early Renaissance; DPS. The story of Henry VIII and Anne Boleyn.

Another Part of the Forest, by Lillian Hellman (drama); 8M, 5W; 1 int.; 1870s; DPS. A despised tyrant, who made a fortune during the Civil War running the blockade, is deposed.

Antigone, by Jean Anouilh (tragedy); 8M, 4W; 1 int.; contemp. adaptation; French. Based on the Greek tragedy by Sophocles, Anouilh's play proves the universal of a classic theme in a struggle between divine law and temporal law.

Arms and the Man, by George Bernard Shaw (comedy); 5M, 3W; 1 or 2 int.; 1 ext.; 19th-century Bulgaria; Baker or French; non-royalty. Raina Petchoff is forced to choose between her "chocolate soldier," the Swiss mercenary, and her former fiancé, a romantic but impractical cavalryman.

Arsenic and Old Lace, by Joseph Kesselring (farce); 11M, 3W; 1 int.; contemp.; DPS. The humorously gruesome story of two sweet old ladies who try to be helpful by gently murdering lonely old men so they won't be lonely anymore.

Auntie Mame, by Jerome Lawrence and Robert E. Lee (comedy); 28M, 12W; simplified staging, numerous ext. and int. sets; 1928 to present; DPS. The slightly madcap adventures of a sparkling, scatter-brained and warm-hearted lady who is devoted to her young nephew. Extensive doubling is possible in the cast.

The Bad Seed, adapted by Maxwell Anderson from W. March's novel (thriller); 7M, 4W; 1 small girl; 1 int.; contemp.; DPS. Little Rhonda Penmark is sweet and charming on the surface, but underneath she is the essence of evil as she literally destroys others through her own jealousy.

The Barretts of Wimpole Street, by Rudolph Besier (romantic comedy); 12M, 5W; 1 int.; mid-Victorian; DPS. Through the inspiration of Robert Browning's love, Elizabeth gains the courage and strength to break away from her tyrannical father and find a new life.

The Beaux' Strategem, by George Farquhar (comedy); 11M, 5W; 1 ext.; 2 int.; (unit set or arena possible); Restoration; public domain. Classic comedy of the transition period, with confused identities, well-made plots, and exuberant lustiness. One of the earliest plays to suggest the use of divorce for an unhappy marriage.

The Beaver Coat, by Gerhart Hauptmann (comedy); 8M, 4W; 2 int.; Germany, late 1800s. Ironic comedy, revolving around Mother Wolff, a washerwoman of good honest local reputation; however, she is a thief. Delicious characters, especially Mrs. Wolff and a stupid police magistrate who bungles at every opportunity. Subtle social and political criticism, set in the Prussian mood.

Belvedere, by Gwen Davenport (comedy); 5M, 4W; 2 children; 1 int.; contemp.; French. A novelist hires himself out as a babysitter and eventually proves that he is a genius.

Bernandine, by Mary Chase (comedy); 13M, 6W; stylized scenery for 5 locales; contemp.; DPS. The whimsical and sometimes pathetic story of a group of teenagers on the verge of becoming adults.

Billy Budd, by Louis O. Coxe and Robert Chapman (from Herman Melville), drama; 22M; 2 int.; 1 ext.; 1798 British Navy; DPS. Caught between the agonizing mandates of the law and every human consideration, ship's officers are compelled to execute an innocent man following the death of the hated Master-at-Arms aboard ship.

The Birds, by Walter Kerr (classic farce); 18M, 2W (sex optional in some roles); 1 ext.; Greek; Catholic University of America Press; non-royalty. A combination of several translations of Aristophanes' old comedy.

Blithe Spirit, by Noel Coward (farce); 2M, 5W; 1 int.; contemp.; French. To gather material for a novel, Charles Condomine arranges to have a seance staged by an eccentric lady medium. Amusing complications arise when the ghost of Charles' first wife appears and mischievously plagues his present marriage.

Born Yesterday, by Garson Kanin (comedy); 5M, 3W, (many extras); 1 int.; Post WW II; DPS. Harry Brock, a junk magnate, is a bullish and crude manipulator. He is in Washington to lobby for legislation to enable him to buy (or steal) all the junk iron left on the WWII battlefields. He decides to give his mistress lessons in manners and literature. Her tutor not only succeeds, but gives her some social conscience as well and they put a stop to Harry's schemes.

The Browning Version, by Terence Rattigan (drama); 4M, 2W; 1 int.; contemp. British; French. A fine, sympathetic study of failure in a brilliant scholar-teacher who must retire because of illness. He is beset by a betraying wife, a thoughtless, patronizing headmaster, and his wife's lover. He gains the courage to stand up to more humiliation through one student whom he perceives to be supportive of him. (Playing time: 70 min., making it a short show.)

The Caine Mutiny Court-Martial, by Herman Wouk (drama); 19M; military court set; contemp. U.S. Navy; French. A young lieutenant is tried for relieving his captain of command during a typhoon on the grounds that the captain was psychopathic.

The Cave Dwellers, by William Saroyan (comedy); 9M, 5W; bare stage; contemp.; French. A group of penniless people with glowing spirits and beautiful memories camp on the stage of an abandoned theatre.

Charley's Aunt, by Brandon Thomas (farce); 6M, 4W; 2 int.; 1 ext.; 1935; French. An Oxford student is forced to impersonate his friend's wealthy aunt from Brazil so that the friend can propose to his sweetheart under proper conditions.

Cheaper by the Dozen, by Perry Clark (comedy); 9M, 7W; 1 int.; early 1900s; Dram. Pub. An efficiency expert runs his family of twelve children with all kinds of time-saving devices. Based on the book by Frank B. Gilbreth, Jr., and Ernestine Gilbreth Carey.

Claudia, by Rose Franken (sentimental comedy); 3M, 5W; 1 int.; contemp.; French. The heart-warming story of a young wife's adjustment to maturity and marriage.

Come Back Little Sheba, by William Inge (drama); 8M, 3W; 1 int.; 1950s; French. A formerly beautiful woman and her reformed drunkard husband are in constant conflict. Her need for attention drives her to aimless conversations with anyone who will listen. Conflict with her husband over a young couple whom she encourages toward romance leads to an attack. He is carried off to an alcoholic ward only to return shortly thereafter to continue his woeful existence. Powerful and difficult challenge.

The Corn Is Green, by Emlyn Williams (comedy); 10M, 5W; extras; 1 int.; early 1900s; DPS. An English spinster school teacher in Wales fights the prejudice of local folk and the wealthy squire as her affection, courage, and wisdom help a promising student win a scholarship.

The Cradle Song, by Gregorio and Maria Martinez Sierra (romantic); 4M, 10W; 2 int.; Spanish milieu, nuns' habits; French. A small child is brought to a convent and grows to maidenhood under the lavish affection of the nuns, who finally give her up when she falls in love.

The Crucible, by Arthur Miller (drama); 10M, 10W; unit set; 1692; DPS. The exciting story of the Puritan purge of witchcraft in old Salem.

The Curious Savage, by John Patrick (comedy); 5M, 6W; 1 int.; contemp.; DPS. Ethel P. Savage, a kind-hearted, wealthy widow, is committed to a sanitarium by her step-children because of her attempts to "give away" the family fortune through her happiness fund. She finds that the inmates have more human kindness than the supposedly sane people outside.

Cyrano de Bergerac, by Edmond Rostand (heroic comedy); 10M, 5W; extras; 2 int.; 3 ext.; 17th-century, France; DPS. The ugly poet-swordsman wins for another man the love he wants for himself.

Dark of the Moon, by Howard Richardson and William Berney (fantasy); 12M, 13W; 3 int.; 4 ext.; late 19th century; French. Dramatization of the mountain witchboy and his love for Barbara Allen. Simplified setting may be used.

Dear Brutus, by J.M. Barrie (comedy); 5M, 7W; 1 int.; 1 ext.; contemp.; French. A man is given a chance to live his life over, and "though poor, he gives his daughter the stars."

Desperate Hours, by Joseph Hayes (melodrama); 10M, 3W; 1 child; multiple int. set; contemp.; French. A suburban family is terrorized for two days by three escaped convicts who take over their home.

Dial "M" for Murder, by Frederick Knott (melodrama); 5M, 1W; 1 int.; contemp.; DPS. A husband hires a scoundrel to strangle his wife, but the murderer is the one who gets killed. The husband then plans to dispose of his wife by having her convicted of the killing, and she is not saved until the final moment of the play.

The Diary of Anne Frank, by Frances Goodrich and Albert Hackett (drama); 5M, 5W; 1 int.; World War II; DPS. The dramatized story of a young Jewish girl and her family, in hiding to escape the Nazis.

Doctor Faustus, by Christopher Marlowe (poetic drama); 36M, 15W; stylized scenery, many special effects; Elizabethan; non-royalty. The classic story of a man who sells his soul to the devil to gain the power of knowledge.

Dream Girl, by Elmer Rice (comedy-fantasy); 25M, 7W; extras; several suggestive settings; contemp.; DPS. A day in the life of a charming but over-imaginative young woman whose extravagant daydreams permit her to escape into a romantic world of unreality. Some doubling in the cast is possible.

Elizabeth the Queen, by Maxwell Anderson (romantic drama); 16M, 7W; extras; 4 int.; 1 ext.; Elizabethan; French. Elizabeth and Essex love each other, but are passionate opponents in the quest for power.

The Enchanted Cottage, by Arthur Pinero (fantasy); 5M, 4W; extras; 1 int.; 1 ext. optional; variable period; Baker. Oliver, a disfigured war hero, and Laura, a homely drudge, marry; through the force of love they believe they have been turned beautiful by a witch.

An Enemy of the People, by Henrik Ibsen (adapted by Arthur Miller) (drama); 10M, 3W; 3 simple int.; late 19th century; DPS. A doctor discovers that the medicinal spring water of his village is contaminated, and is shocked to find that his townspeople look upon him as a dangerous crank for having made the discovery.

Ethan Frome, by Owen and Donald Davis (from Edith Wharton's novel) (drama); 7M, 4W; 2 int.; several simple ext.; 1900; DPS. The stark tragedy of a New England man who falls in love with the young woman who has come to take care of his semi-invalid wife.

The Eve of St. Mark, by Maxwell Anderson (drama); 13M, 8W; 1 curtain set w/prop changes; World War II; Dramatic Pub. On the Eve of St. Mark, condemned G.I.'s in the Philippines see and talk to those they love back home.

Everybody Loves Opal, by John Patrick (comedy); 4M, 2W; 1 int.; contemp.; DPS. Opal is a friendly middle-aged recluse who collects things (old newspapers, broken furniture, used tea bags). She radiates kindness, affection, and gratitude as an unsavory trio plots unsuccessfully to murder her for insurance benefits.

Everyman, anonymous (morality play); 11M, 6W; variable setting; 16th century; French; non-royalty. Popular old-English religious play. Roles may be cast all male or all female.

Family Portrait, by Lenore Coffee and William Cowen (Biblical drama); 12M, 10W; 1 int.; 3 ext.; Biblical; French. The effect of the life of Christ upon the common people of His time, shown during His later years and after His death.

The Farmer's Daughter, adapted (from the movie) by F. Andrew Leslie (comedy); 11M, 3W; 1 int.; contemp.; DPS. The captivating story of the unspoiled girl from the country who triumphs over the sophisticated politicians of the big city.

Father of the Bride, by Caroline Francke (comedy); 11M, 7W; extras; 1 int.; contemp.; DPS. A "simple wedding" mushrooms to overflow proportions, with many humorous complications.

George Washington Slept Here, by Moss Hart and George S. Kaufman (comedy); 9M, 8W; 1 int.; contemp.; DPS. The trials and tribulations of the Newton family, who move into a country home which has "a few minor inconveniences" (for example no water, no lights, broken stairs, open roof, etc.).

The Girls in 509, by Howard Teichmann (political satire); 9M, 3W; 1 int.; contemp.; French. While an unfashionable hotel in New York is being remodeled, a pair of hermit ladies is discovered in one of the back suites, where they have been since 1932—when Herbert Hoover lost the election. The play pokes fun at both political parties.

The Glass Menagerie, by Tennessee Williams (drama); 2M, 2W; unit set; contemp.; DPS. The now-classic tale of the Wingfield family in the dingy St. Louis apartment and the arrival of the gentleman caller.

Golden Fleecing, by Lorenzo Semple, Jr. (farce); 11M, 2W; 1 int.; contemp.; French. Young Navy men concoct a fantastic scheme to break the bank of Venice by beating the odds on a roulette wheel.

Goodbye, My Fancy, by Fay Kanin (comedy); 8M, 12W; 1 int.; contemp.; French. A liberal congresswoman returns to her old school as an honorary visitor with an appeal for common sense in facing the horrors of war.

The Great Sebastians, by Howard Lindsay and Russel Crouse (melodramatic comedy); 15M, 6W; 2 int.; contemp. and Russian military; DPS. A man and his wife, a famous mind-reading act, fall into the clutches of the Communist leaders in Czechoslovakia.

Guest in the House, by Hagar Wilde and Dale Eunson (drama); 6M, 8W; 1 int.; contemp.; French. An invited guest with a heart ailment appeals to the protective instincts of both men and women, but it soon becomes apparent that at heart she is selfish, conniving, and generally cruel as she brings scandal, fear, and disunity to the Proctor household.

The Happiest Millionaire, by Kyle Crichton (from the book by Cordelia Biddle) (farce); 9M, 6W; 1 int.; World War I; DPS. The wealthy and eccentric Anthony Biddle of Philadelphia almost wrecks his daughter's forthcoming marriage to a wealthy young tobacco heir because he hates to see the family circle broken up.

The Happy Time, by Samuel Taylor (comedy); 8M, 4W; 2 int.; 1920s (French Canada); DPS. A 13-year-old boy learns through warmth and humor what it is "truly to be a man."

Harvey, by Mary Chase (comedy); 6M, 6W; 2 int.; contemp.; DPS. The warmly humorous story of Elwood P. Dowd and his best friend, an invisible white rabbit, 6 feet tall.

The Hasty Heart, by John Patrick (comedy-drama); 8M, 1W; 1 int.; World War II; DPS. A wounded Scotch soldier with an extremely independent spirit learns, during the last few weeks of his life, the great lesson of love for his neighbor.

Hay Fever, by Noel Coward (comedy); 4M, 5W; 1 int.; 1920s; French. Weekend guests are bewildered by the antics of a retired actress and her ultra-Bohemian family.

Heaven Can Wait, by Harry Segall (comedy-fantasy); 12M, 6W; 1 int., with 2 side or curtain scenes; contemp.; DPS. After much trouble, Joe Pendleton returns to the earth from the hereafter and wins the girl.

The Heiress, by Ruth and Augustus Goetz (from Henry James's novel) (drama); 3M, 6W; 1 int.; 1850; DPS. A shy and plain young girl falls desperately in love with a fortune-hunter, but learns to reject him when his motive becomes obvious.

He Who Gets Slapped, by Leonid Andreyev (drama); 13M, 7W; 1 int.; Circus environment of any period; French. An upper class gentleman, disillusioned with society, joins a circus and becomes the clown who always is the one to be slapped. He falls in love with Consuela, the bareback rider, but it turns out that he has a rival. A tragic picture of man's frustrated potential for happiness ends with his poisoning of Consuela and his own suicide. A theatrical and powerful play.

Holiday for Lovers, by Ronald Alexander (comedy); 4M, 5W; 4 int.; contemp.; DPS. A family from Minnesota finds pleasure, love, and understanding on a vacation in Europe.

The Imaginary Invalid, by Molière (trans. by M. Stone) (classic farce); 8M, 4W; 1 int.; 17th-century France; French; non-royalty. The story of a hypochondriac and his cure.

The Importance of Being Earnest, by Oscar Wilde (farce); 5M, 4W; 1 or 2 int.; 1 ext.; Victorian; French; non-royalty. Much confusion and humor result from two double identities.

Inherit the Wind, by Jerome Lawrence and Robert E. Lee (drama); 21M, 6W; extras; unit set; 1920s; DPS. Dramatization of the famous Scopes trial on evolution in which Bryan and Darrow were opposing lawyers.

The Innocents, by William Archibald (melodrama); 2M, 4W; 1 int.; 19th century; French. Dramatization of Henry James's story, "The Turn of the Screw," in which the souls of two orphaned children are corrupted by evil spirits.

I Remember Mama, by John Van Druten (adapted from K. Forbes' novel) (comedy); 9M, 13W; unit set; 1900–1910; DPS. The heartwarming story of an immigrant family in San Francisco.

J.B., by Archibald MacLeish (verse drama); 12M, 9W; 1 int.; contemp.; French. The Pulitzer Prize–winning play based on the Book of Job, dealing with the problems of man's relationship to God in an era of cruel injustices.

Joan of Lorraine, by Maxwell Anderson (romantic drama); 18M, 5W; bare stage with scenic pieces; contemp. (some medieval); DPS. The meaning of faith today is shown through parallel action to a rehearsal for Joan of Arc.

John Brown's Body, by Stephen Vincent Benet (dramatic reading); 2M, 1W, plus chorus; costumes optional; DPS. A highly dramatic epic poem of the Civil War.

Johnny Belinda, by Elmer Harris (drama); 16M, 7W; unit set; contemp.; Nova Scotia; DPS. The powerful story of the trials and tribulations of a deaf-mute, rich with truth and a timeless message of human understanding.

Junior Miss, by Jerome Chodorov and Joseph Fields (from the book by Sally Benson) (comedy); 11M, 6W; 1 int.; contemp.; DPS. One of the most popular plays about the antics and imaginative schemings of teenagers.

Kind Lady, by Edward Chodorov (from a story by Hugh Walpole) (melodrama); 6M, 8W; 1 int.; contemp.; French. A dignified and aristocratic woman is gradually surrounded by a family of diabolically clever crooks who almost succeed in convincing all who know her that the kind lady is hopelessly insane.

King of Hearts, by Jean Kerr and Eleanor Brooke (comedy); 6M, 2W; 2 children, 1 dog; contemp.; DPS. The witty, wry treatment of the familiar triangle, one of whom is the world's foremost egoist.

Ladies in Retirement, by Edward Percy and Reginald Denham (mystery); 1M, 6W; 1 int.; contemp.; DPS. Devotion to her dependent sister leads Ellen Creed to murder.

Lady Precious Stream, by S. I. Hsiung (Chinese play); 5M, 5W; extras; conventional Chinese scene and costumes; French. A romantic drama of love, fidelity, treachery, and poetry in the colorful Chinese manner.

The Lady's Not for Burning, by Christopher Fry (poetic comedy); 8M, 3W; 1 int.; 15th century; DPS. The romantic entanglements of a man who wants to be hanged and a woman who doesn't.

The Lark, by Jean Anouilh (adapted by Lillian Hellman) (drama); 15M, 7W; 1 formal set with suggestive scene pieces; medieval; DPS. The trial of Joan of Arc, with flashbacks depicting the events leading to her martyrdom.

The Late Christopher Bean, by Sidney Howard (comedy); 5M, 4W; 1 int.; contemp.; French. A New England family discovers they had given refuge to a famous artist when his death brings recognition to his paintings. Only the maid had understood and appreciated him while he was alive—and she had been married to him.

The Late George Apley, by John P. Marquand and George S. Kaufman (comedy-drama); 8M, 8W; 2 int.; early 1900s; DPS. A young man and a young woman strive heroically to break away from the shackles of family and tradition.

The Leading Lady, by Ruth Gordon (comedy-drama); 11M, 9W; 2 int.; 1900; DPS. A picturesque play about the American theatre at the turn of the century.

Life with Father, by Howard Lindsay and Russel Crouse (comedy); 8M, 8W; 1 int.; 1880s; DPS. Clarence Day and his wife Vinnie get everyone involved in the tremendous struggle over a proper baptism for father.

Life with Mother, by Howard Lindsay and Russel Crouse (comedy); 8M, 8W; 2 int.; 1880s; DPS. A sequel to *Life with Father,* in which Mother, after 17 years of marriage, insists upon having an engagement ring of her own.

Liliom, by Ferenc Molnar (fantasy); 17M, 5W; extras; 1 int.; 4 ext.; contemp. Budapest; French. The tender and moving story of a shiftless ne'er-do-well and bully who is granted a brief return to earth, after he has killed himself, to prove that he can do one good deed.

The Little Foxes, by Lillian Hellman (drama); 6M, 4W; 1 int.; late 19th century; DPS. The dramatic entanglements of the despotic Hubbard family as they vie for money, power, and position.

Little Moon of Alban, by James Costigan (drama); 10M, 8W; unit set; Ireland in 1920s; French. An eloquent plea for healing power of faith and forgiveness, expressed through the lives of men and women in the Black and Tan conflict.

Look Back in Anger, by John Osborne, (drama); 3M, 2W; 1 int.; Postwar England; Dramatic Pub. One of the protest plays centered around a young beat generation couple. A series of events results in a violent quarrel and the wife leaves the husband. She returns later, ill and destitute, and they are reunited by the fact that they need each other.

Look Homeward Angel, by Ketti Frings (adapted from Thomas Wolfe) (drama); 10M, 9W; 2 ext. and insert; 1917; French. Dramatization of Thomas Wolfe's autobiographical novel of the Gant family.

The Loud Red Patrick, by John Boruff (from the novel by Ruth McKenney) (comedy); 4M, 5W; 1 int.; 1912; French. Patrick Flannigan is a firm believer in democracy and wants all family problems settled by parliamentary principles, but the system backfires when his 17-year-old daughter wants to get married.

Love for Love, by William Congreve (comedy); 10M, 6W; 4 int. (sets that can be combined by use of wing and drop or unit); Restoration comedy; public domain. The typical comedy of errors, complicated with numerous plots and subplots, and memorable characters. Very witty dialogue revealing misguided decisions, feigned insanity, inheritance schemes, lovers' byplay, and naive society folk.

The Madwoman of Chaillot, by Jean Giraudoux (comic fable); 17M, 8W; extras; 1 int.; 1 ext.; stylized costumes; DPS. The madwoman cleverly turns the tables on thieves who are greedy for worldly goods and power.

The Magnificent Yankee, by Emmet Lavery (comedy); 15M, 2W; 1 int.; 1902–1933; French. The story of a marriage that lasted 57 years: the marriage of Justice Oliver Wendell Holmes and his wife.

A Majority of One, by Leonard Spiegelgass (comedy); 6M, 8W; 4 int.; contemp. and Japanese; French. A Jewish widow and a distinguished Japanese gentleman show that intolerance stems from a lack of understanding.

The Male Animal, by James Thurber and Elliott Nugent (comedy); 8M, 5W; int.; contemp.; French. The scintillating story of a mild professor of English who stirs up a peck of trouble when he announces that he will read in class a letter by a suspected Communist.

The Man, by Mel Dinelli (drama); 5M, 2W; 1 int.; contemp.; DPS. Mrs. Gillis is imprisoned in her own home, and finally murdered, by a disarmingly charming maniac.

The Man Who Came to Dinner, by Moss Hart and George S. Kaufman (comedy); 15M, 9W; extras; 1 int.; contemp.; DPS. Sheridan Whiteside, an irascible critic and sophisticate, is confined by injury to the Stanley home, where he receives weird visitors and strange gifts.

The Matchmaker, by Thornton Wilder (farce); 9M, 7W; 4 int.; 1880; French. A rich merchant hires a female marriage broker to arrange a marriage for him and ends by being snagged by the woman herself.

Member of the Wedding, by Carson McCullers (drama); 6M, 7W; unit set; contemp.; DPS. A study of the loneliness of an over-imaginative young girl in Georgia.

The Miracle Worker, by William Gibson (drama); 7M, 7W; unit set; 1882; French. The dramatization of Ann Sullivan's emotional struggle to teach the blind and deaf Helen Keller.

The Mousetrap, by Agatha Christie (melodrama); 5M, 3W; 1 int.; contemp.; French. A group of strangers, one of whom is a murderer, is stranded in a boarding house during a snow storm.

Mr. Pim Passes By, by A. A. Milne (comedy); 3M, 4W; 1 int.; contemp.; French. A second wife brings her present husband to terms by using mistaken information that her first husband is still alive.

Mrs. McThing, by Mary Chase (fantasy); 9M (1 child); 10W (1 child); 2 int.; contemp.; DPS. A whimsical tale of the education of Mrs. Howard V. Larue III by her nine-year-old son and a little witchgirl.

Murder Has Been Arranged, by Emlyn Williams (melodrama); 4M, 5W; 1 int.; contemp.; French. A nephew tricks his rich uncle into signing a suicide confession before he murders him.

My Sister Eileen, by Joseph Fields and Jerome Chodorov (comedy); 21M, 6W; 1 int.; contemp.; DPS. Two girls from Ohio try to "make their mark" in New York.

My Three Angels, by Sam and Bella Spewack (comedy); 7M, 3W; 1 int.; 1910; DPS. Three convicts in French Guiana become the good angels of a sadly harassed household.

The Night Is My Enemy, by Fred Carmichael (suspense drama); 5M, 5W; 1 int.; 1900; French. A blind girl finds herself up against a mentally unbalanced killer.

Night Must Fall, by Emlyn Williams (suspense drama); 4M, 5W; 1 int.; contemp.; French. A young but pleasant psychopath menaces an older lady and her niece.

No Time for Sergeants, by Ira Levin (comedy); 34M, 3W; unit set; contemp.; DPS. A good-natured hillbilly comes in conflict with the Air Force way of doing things. Casting and uniforms might provide problems for some groups.

On Borrowed Time, by Paul Osborn (fantasy); 11M, 3W; 1 ext.; contemp.; DPS. A young boy and his grandmother hold Death captive in a tree.

One Foot in Heaven, by Anne Coulter Martens (from Hartzell Spence's book); 8M, 10W; 11 int.; 1910; Dram. Pub. An Iowa minister moves into a parish under the worst possible conditions and finishes by dedicating his new church.

Onions in the Stew, by Betty MacDonald (comedy); 7M, 11W; 1 int.; contemp.; Dram. Pub. An adventurous family samples the delights and headaches of country living on an island in Puget Sound.

Our Hearts Were Young and Gay, by Cornelia Otis Skinner and Emily Kimbrough (dramatized by Jean Kerr) (comedy); 7M, 10W; unit set; 1920; Dram. Pub. Two independent girls face typical tourist problems on a trip to Europe.

Our Town, by Thornton Wilder (drama); 17M, 7W; extras; bare stage; 1900 costumes; French. The townspeople and two youngsters in love are followed through a series of flashbacks and glimpses into the world beyond. This play was a winner of the Pulitzer Prize.

Out of the Frying Pan, by Francis Swann (comedy); 7M, 5W; 1 int.; contemp.; French. Six stagestruck youngsters try to meet a producer who lives in the same apartment building.

Papa Is All, by Patterson Greene (comedy); 3M, 3W; 1 int.; contemp.; French. A Pennsylvania Dutch family is ruled tyrannically by the father, whose influence over the family is finally broken.

Picnic, by William Inge (drama); 3M, 6W; 1 ext.; contemp.; DPS. A story in which a widow sees her daughter make the same mistakes she made in her own life. Two daughters are influenced by the same young man, who breaks the heart of one and then seduces and leaves with the other. Some clearly and poignantly drawn characterizations in a drab midwestern small town.

The Playboy of the Western World, by John M. Synge (comedy); 7M, 5W; 1 int.; Irish contemp.; French. Christopher Mahon finds himself a hero after he has supposedly killed his father, but the old man turns up to spoil his new position.

The Potting Shed, by Graham Greene (mystery-drama); 6M, 5W; 3 int.; contemp. English; French. The prodigal son returns home to his father's death and coldness from his mother. Some strange event has taken place in his own life that he cannot identify, other than it took place in the potting shed, when he was fourteen. Through some detective work he discovers that he hanged himself there and was resurrected, thus destroying his father's atheistic beliefs as well as his priest-uncle's faith.

Pygmalion, by George Bernard Shaw (comedy); 6M, 6W; 3 int.; 2 ext.; 1900; French. The story of a phonetics expert who wagers that he can transform a flower girl with a cockney accent into a lady and pass her off in high society.

The Rainmaker, by N. Richard Nash (comedy); 6M, 1W; 1 int.; Western contemp.; French. A con man promises to bring rain to a drought-struck ranch for $100, but ends up bringing much more to those who live there.

Raisin in the Sun, by Lorraine Hansberry (drama); 7M, 3W; 1 int.; contemp.; French. A poor African American family in Chicago achieves greater maturity and dignity as its members struggle to use $10,000 insurance money wisely.

Remains to Be Seen, by Howard Lindsay and Russel Crouse (mystery-comedy); 16M, 3W; 1 int.; contemp.; DPS. A jazz drummer and a band singer are caught up in the search for the killer of a rich and unmourned reformer.

The Remarkable Mr. Pennypacker, by Liam O'Brian (comedy); 10M, 4W; 6 child.; 1 int.; 1890; French. A free-thinking businessman maintains one family in Wilmington, Delaware, and another in Philadelphia, until the paths of the two families cross.

Ring Around the Moon, by Jean Anouilh (comedy); 6M, 7W; 1 ext.; contemp.; DPS. A satirical comedy about love.

The Rivals, by Richard Brinsley Sheridan (comedy); 9M, 4W; 12 scenes in various places (unit); 18th century; public domain. High comedy and confusion of identities showcasing some of the most memorable characters: Mrs. Malaprop, Anthony Absolute, Bob Acres, et al. Marvelous matchmaking and comic incidents. A classic.

The Royal Family, by George S. Kaufman and Edna Ferber (comedy); 11M, 6W; 1 int.; contemp.; French. The Cavendish family, led by Fanny, has dominated the American stage for years; the granddaughter first rebels, and then follows tradition.

Romanoff and Juliet, by Peter Ustinov (comedy); 9M, 4W; unit set; contemp.; DPS. The son of a Russian diplomat and the daughter of an American diplomat fall in love in a small mythical European country, with a happier outcome than that of Shakespeare's lovers.

R. U. R., by Karel Capek (drama); 13M, 4W; 2 int.; contemp.; French. Highly developed robots take over the earth and kill their masters; then love develops between two of the humanized robots and mankind is about to start afresh.

Sabrina Fair, by Samuel Taylor (comedy); 7M, 7W; 1 ext.; contemp.; DPS. Linus, a cynical young tycoon, finally realizes that he is in love with the well-educated daughter of the family chauffeur.

Saint Joan, by George Bernard Shaw (drama); 25M, 2W; drapes suggested; medieval; Baker. This is Shaw's treatment of the Joan of Arc story.

Seven Keys to Baldpate, by George M. Cohan (mystery); 9M, 4W; 1 int.; contemp.; French. A writer goes to a supposedly deserted mountain inn in search of a plot and runs into a mystery involving an assortment of colorful characters.

She Stoops to Conquer, by Oliver Goldsmith (comedy); 15M, 4W; 3 int.; 1 ext.; 18th century; French; non-royalty. The heroine finds herself posing as a servant in order to win the hand of the man she loves.

The Silver Cord, by Sidney Howard (drama); 2M, 4W; 2 int.; contemp.; French. A mother breaks up the engagement of one son and almost destroys the marriage of the other in an effort to keep them emotionally tied to her.

The Silver Whistle, by Robert E. McEnroe (comedy); 10M, 5W; 1 ext.; contemp.; DPS. An amiable con man and tramp goes to live in a home for the aged. By the time he leaves he has changed the lives and warmed the hearts of all those with whom he has come in contact.

The Skin of Our Teeth, by Thornton Wilder (fantasy); 5M, 5W; many extras; 1 int.; 1 ext.; various costumes; French. The satiric story of the Antrobus family down through the ages, from prehistoric to modern times. The Pulitzer Prize was awarded this play.

The Solid Gold Cadillac, by Howard Teichmann and George S. Kaufman (comedy); 11M, 6W; various simple sets; contemp.; DPS. A little old lady who owns a few shares in a large corporation ends up in control of it when all the shareholders revolt against the incompetence of the directors, whom she has exposed.

The Spiral Staircase, by F. Andrew Leslie (suspense drama); 4M, 4W; 1 int.; contemp.; DPS. The young companion of a bedridden woman finds that she is the next intended victim of an unbalanced killer.

Sunrise at Campobello, by Dore Schary (drama); 19M, 5W; 3 int.; contemp.; DPS. The play covers the period in Franklin D. Roosevelt's life between August 1921, when he was stricken with polio while on vacation, and June 1924, when he was able to stand on his feet long enough to nominate Al Smith for President at the Democratic convention.

Tall Story, by Howard Lindsay and Russel Crouse (comedy); 22M, 8W; simple interiors; contemp.; DPS. The star basketball player at a small college finds his life complicated by the faculty, his girlfriend, and some crooks who want him to throw the big game.

The Teahouse of the August Moon, John Patrick (comedy); 18M, 8W; 3 child.; 1 goat; several sets; army and Asian costumes; DPS. An officer in the Army of Occupation on Okinawa finds himself running various nonregulation enterprises, including a teahouse and a brandy factory, when he tries to teach democracy to the natives and make the economy self-supporting. Pulitzer Prize winner.

Ten Little Indians, by Agatha Christie (suspense drama); 8M, 3W; 1 int.; contemp.; French. A group of people who are not acquainted with each other find when they arrive for a house party at an island estate that they also do not know their host. One by one they are murdered until only two are left.

Thieves' Carnival, by Jean Anouilh (comedy); 10M, 3W; unit set; contemp.; French. Three thieves invade a palatial home where two attractive girls live, and a romance blooms between one of the girls and the youngest thief.

Three Men on a Horse, by John Cecil Holm and George Abbott (comedy); 11M, 4W; 3 int.; contemp.; DPS. A timid little man in a low-paying job finds that he has a strange knack for picking winners at the race track; in the process he falls in with three professional gamblers.

Thurber Carnival, by James Thurber (comic revue); 5M, 4W (more if desired); number of simple scenes; variety of costumes; French. Sketches taken from favorite short stories and cartoons of James Thurber.

Tiger at the Gates, adapted from Jean Giraudoux by Christopher Fry (drama); 15M, 7W; platform stage; French. The ancient Greek legends are retold, and Troy is destroyed.

Time Remembered, by Jean Anouilh (comedy); 13M, 2W; 1 int.; 2 ext.; contemp.; French. Prince Albert Troubiscoi discovers a new love while striving to hold on to the memory of his lost love.

Twelve Angry Men, by Sherman L. Sergel (from the TV play by Reginald Rose) (drama); 15M; 1 int.; contemp.; Dram. Pub. The jury in a murder trial struggles to reach a just verdict. Also available as *Twelve Angry Women,* with an all-female cast.

Two Blind Mice, by Samuel Spewack (comedy); 14M, 4W; 1 int.; contemp.; DPS. Two nice old ladies run a forgotten bureau, the Office of Medicinal Herbs, which once was part of the Department of Agriculture in Washington.

Under Milk Wood, by Dylan Thomas (tragi-comedy); 29M, 28W; (doubling and tripling desirable); usually done as readers theatre; contemp. Welsh; French. A series of vignettes, in which we see the goings-on of a small Welsh sea town through the eyes of interrelated characters: Capt. Cat, the blind seaman who rings the church bell and thinks of his mates lost at sea; the postman's wife who steams open letters to keep abreast of the local affairs; Polly Garter, the town tart; and many others.

The Unexpected Guest, by Agatha Christie (suspense drama); 7M, 3W; 1 int.; contemp.; French. A man is murdered on a British country estate and the most obvious suspect is a man who was reported dead two years before.

Visit to a Small Planet, by Gore Vidal (comedy); 8M, 2W; 1 int.; contemp.; DPS. A visitor from a "more advanced" planet comes to earth to view the Civil War. Having missed that war he tries to start one for his own amusement.

What Every Woman Knows, by J. M. Barrie (comedy); 7M, 4W; 4 int.; 1900; French. An ambitious young Scot marries a plain woman in exchange for the opportunity for an education, and later discovers that he loves her.

The Wild Duck, by Henrik Ibsen (tragedy); 9M, 3W; 2 int.; 1800s. A poor family of a photographer lives simply in a deluded dream world that becomes shattered by an idealistic do-gooder who brings "the truth" to the family, ultimately causing tragedy. One of the earliest examples of social criticism and one of Ibsen's most powerful plays.

The Winslow Boy, by Terence Rattigan (drama); 7M, 4W; 1 int.; 1900; DPS. A boy is unjustly expelled from an English governmental school and his family fights the case up through the bureaucratic channels.

Witness for the Prosecution, by Agatha Christie (suspense drama); 17M, 5W; 8 extras; 2 int.; contemp.; French. A man is tried for the murder of a rich old lady with whom he has spent many evenings.

The World of Sholom Aleichem, by Arnold Perl (comedy-fantasy); three short plays; total 19M, 10W; 19th-century Europe; DPS. These three plays, which can be done separately as well as together, depict the life of Jewish people in Europe in the last century.

Years Ago, by Ruth Gordon (comedy); 4M, 5W; 1 int.; early 1900s; DPS. A girl finally gets the permission of her parents to go to New York and try for a stage career.

Yellow Jack, by Sidney Howard (drama); 26M, 1W; unit set; the army about 1900; DPS. A dramatization of the experiments in Cuba which led to the discovery of the cure for yellow fever.

You Can't Take It With You, by Moss Hart and George S. Kaufman (comedy); 9M, 7W; 1 int.; contemp.; DPS. The Sycamores, a family of happy individuals, find themselves in hilarious conflict with the conformist Kirbys.

Play Publishers and Addresses

Baker Plays
100 Chauncey St.
Boston, MA 02111

The Dramatic Publishing Company
123 Sharp Hill Rd.
Wilton, CT 06897

Dramatists Play Service, Inc.
440 Park Avenue South
New York, NY 10016

Samuel French, Inc.
45 W. 25th St.
New York, NY 10010

Index

Theatre-in-the-round, 19
Thespis, 2
This Piece of Land (Rivers), 75–79
Thrust stage, 19
Tone, 42
Tragedian, 2
Tragoedia, 8
Tragedy, 8
   Greek, 3
Tragic flaw, 8
Tragic hero, 8
Trifles (Glaspell), 6, 70–75
Trilogy, 3
20th century drama, 5–6
Typecasting, 32

U

Upstage, 20

V

Valdez, Luis, 6
Vaudeville, 5
Vocal characteristics, 41–44
   inflection, 42
   pitch, 42
   rate, 43
   tone, 42

W

Wasserstein, Wendy, 6
Webber, Andrew Lloyd, 6
Wilde, Oscar, 5, 68–70
Wilder, Thornton, 39
Wilson, August, 6
Working rehearsals, 50–51

Y

You Can't Take It With You, 24

Acknowledgments

Actor's Equity employment statistics reprinted by permission of Dick Moore and Associates, New York City.

Excerpts from "Shakespeare Through the Stages" and "Frog Songs" by Jean Battlo, reprinted by permission of the author.

Excerpt from "Trifles" by Susan Glaspell, originally produced in 1916, copyright 1951 by Walter H. Baker Company. Reprinted with permission of Baker Plays, 1100 Chauncey St., Boston, MA 02111.

Excerpt from "The Open Scene As a Directing Experience" by Wandalie Henshaw, originally published in *The Educational Theater Journal*, Volume XXI, October, 1969. Reprinted by permission of The Johns Hopkins University Press.

Excerpt from "The Sound of a Voice," copyright © 1990 by David Henry Hwang, from FOB AND OTHER PLAYS by David Henry Hwang. Used by permission of Dutton Signet, a division of Penguin Books USA Inc.

Excerpt from "Carwash" by Louis Phillips, originally published in *CrazyQuilt*. Reprinted by permission of the author.

Excerpt from "This Piece of Land" by Lou Rivers. Reprinted by permission of the author.

Excerpt from "Black Elk Speaks" by Christopher Sergel. Reprinted by permission of The Dramatic Publishing Company, Wilton, Connecticut. The play was adapted from the book by the same title by John G. Neihardt © 1979, University of Nebraska Press.

Excerpt from Scene V from THE MISANTHROPE BY MOLIÈRE, copyright © 1955, 1954, and renewed 1983, 1982 by Richard Wilbur, reprinted by permission of Harcourt Brace & Company.

Excerpt from MISER AND OTHER PLAYS by Molière, translated by John Wood. Copyright © 1953 by Viking Penguin, reprinted by permission of Penguin & Co., London.

Photo Credits

Jeff Ellis, pages 1, 41, and 48; Courtesy of Fairmont Senior High School, Fairmont, West Virginia, pages 17, 26 and 32; Courtesy of Maine Township High School West, Des Plaines, Illinois, page 52.